FEW OTHER BOOKS BY THIS AUTHOR

Copyright © 2025 by Osoria Asibor
All rights reserved.

No part of this publication may be reproduced, stored in a retrieval system, or transmitted in any form or by any means—electronic, mechanical, photocopying, recording, or otherwise—without the prior written permission of the author, except for brief quotations used in critical articles or reviews.

For permissions or inquiries, contact:
standardwordz@gmail.com
ISBN: 978-1-998308-18-7
First Edition – 2025
Printed in Canada
Published by Osoria Asibor

This is a work of fiction. Names, characters, places, and incidents either are the product of the author's imagination or are used fictitiously. Any resemblance to actual persons, living or dead, events, or locales is entirely coincidental.

Cover Design: Osoria Asibor
Interior Layout: Osoria Asibor

Acknowledgments

I give all glory to God for the grace, inspiration, and strength to birth this story. Every word written here is a testimony of His faithfulness and wisdom.

To my dear wife and children—thank you for your unwavering love and patience through countless hours of writing, reflection, and late-night edits. Your support is the wind beneath my wings.

To the many young men and women whose life stories and struggles echo the themes in this book—you are seen. Your pain, growth, and choices matter. May this story help you find hope and healing.

To my mentors, spiritual leaders, and prayer partners—thank you for speaking life into me, even when I doubted the calling.

And to every reader of *The Choices We Make*—thank you for opening your heart to this journey. May it stir reflection, compassion, and a deeper appreciation for the power of our decisions.

— **Osoria Asibor**

Table of Contents
Chapter One: The Beginning..................9
- Samuel and Grace's journey from Nigeria to Canada.
- The birth of the twins, Peter and Paul.
- Early childhood - Observations of their distinct personalities.
- Family life: Prayers, storytelling, and foundational values.
- Introduction to their home and neighborhood.
- Cultural differences and efforts to integrate into Canadian society.
- Challenges faced by Samuel and Grace as immigrants.

Chapter Two: Footsteps in a New Land.......45
- Peter and Paul's transition from toddlerhood to elementary school.
- School experiences: Making friends, adapting to a new culture, and facing subtle discrimination.
- Academic performance and parental expectations.
- Peer influences and early signs of divergence in interests.
- Grace's involvement in the church and introducing the boys to Christian teachings.

- Samuel's work experiences, sacrifices, and hopes for his children.
- Community events and cultural gatherings.
- The twins' differing reactions to church and community activities.

Chapter Three: Brothers Apart............83
- Pre-teen years and emerging individuality.
- Peter's growing curiosity and rebelliousness.
- Paul's steady faith and developing leadership qualities.
- Family outings, interactions, and misunderstandings.
- Conflicts between the brothers over values and expectations.
- Samuel and Grace's efforts to nurture both sons despite their differences.
- Introduction of friendships that influence Peter and Paul in opposing ways.
- Moments of connection and alienation between the brothers.

Chapter Four: The Call of Rebellion........115
- Peter's entrance into adolescence: Increased defiance and questioning of authority.
- Paul's deepening commitment to his faith and academic excellence.
- Peter's attraction to peers who encourage his rebelliousness.

- Samuel's frustration and attempts to guide Peter back on track.
- Grace's quiet prayers and maternal worry.
- The role of the church community in shaping Paul's values.
- Peter's rejection of religious teachings.
- Increasing tension between the brothers and their parents.

Chapter Five: The Road Less Traveled.......143
- Peter's first major act of rebellion: A critical turning point.
- Paul's achievements in school and church.
- Samuel and Grace's struggle to balance their hopes for both sons.
- Peter's exposure to harmful influences.
- Paul's growing sense of responsibility within the church.
- Conversations between Samuel and Grace about their sons' future.
- The introduction of mentors or negative influencers for each brother.
- Peter's increasing resentment toward Paul's success.

Chapter Six: Rising Tensions...................171
- Family conflicts come to a head.
- Paul's internal struggle with balancing love and resentment toward Peter.

- Samuel's harsh words and regrets.
- Grace's attempts at reconciliation.
- Peter's destructive behaviors intensify.
- Paul's journey toward becoming a youth leader.
- A significant event that widens the rift between the brothers.
- Samuel's health beginning to fail under stress.

Chapter Seven: A Divergence of Paths......197
- Paul's academic success and spiritual growth.
- Peter's increasing detachment from family and faith.
- Grace's heartbreak and persistence in prayer.
- Samuel's frustration turning into resignation.
- Paul's first encounter with love and romantic relationships.
- Peter's own relationship entanglements and poor decisions.
- Attempts at reconciliation that only deepen the divide.
- Peter's decision to leave home or take a destructive path.

Chapter Eight: The Breaking Point.........221
- The climax of the volume: A devastating fallout between Peter and Paul.
- Samuel and Grace's heartbreak as their sons' paths fully diverge.

- The consequences of Peter's choices becoming evident.
- Paul's struggle to forgive and remain steadfast.
- Grace's unwavering faith despite her grief.

Chapter One:

The Beginning

Samuel and Grace's Journey from Nigeria to Canada

Samuel Okafor was a man forged in the fires of Lagos—sharp, diligent, and quietly ambitious. Though life in Nigeria demanded resilience, he had carved out a measure of stability in the bustling heart of the city, earning respect in the logistics industry and providing a modest but steady life for himself and Grace, his devoted wife. But even stability can feel like stagnation when danger lurks at every street corner, and a ceiling hangs low above dreams too wide to fit.

Grace, grounded in faith and vision, was the first to speak the unspeakable. "Samuel, I believe there is more. Not just for us—but for the children we've not yet met."

Samuel, skeptical yet weary, wrestled with the idea. Migration meant leaving everything familiar—family, culture, career, identity. But the thought of raising children in safety, giving them opportunities he never had, began to weigh heavier than his fears.

After years of prayer, applications, setbacks, and small miracles, the doors opened. Visas in hand, faith in heart, and little else in their pockets, they boarded a flight to Canada. The cold slap of

Winnipeg's winter was the first shock. But it would not be the last.

Their new apartment in the North End was a far cry from what they'd imagined. Cracked walls, creaky plumbing, and a biting draft that laughed at their space heater. Still, Grace looked around with awe. "God has provided," she said. "This is a beginning."

Samuel buried himself in work—anything to keep them afloat. He cleaned offices, stocked shelves, and drove taxis. Once a respected manager, he now scrubbed floors without acknowledgment. Each paycheck was a silent reminder of how far he had fallen in the eyes of society.

Grace became a home care assistant. Though the work was demanding, her compassion found a place to bloom. Her faith deepened, her worship louder, her joy strangely undiminished.

Samuel, however, grew quieter.

"I feel invisible," he confessed one night. "Stripped of who I was. Like I don't matter anymore."

Grace took his hand. "You're not invisible to me. Or to God. We are in the wilderness, yes—but He is still leading."

They found a small Nigerian church where hymns sounded familiar, and prayers echoed like home. Grace flourished in that community. Samuel struggled to believe again.

Yet, in the midst of hard beginnings, they found reasons to hold on. Friendships formed. Laughter returned in quiet waves. And then came the news that changed everything.

"I am pregnant," Grace whispered one evening, tears filling her eyes.

Samuel froze. Then smiled. Then wept.

A child. A future. A reason to keep building.

What they didn't yet know was that God had doubled the blessing.

Twins.

And with them, a story would begin—one of brotherhood, rebellion, redemption, and the enduring weight of the choices we make.

The Birth of the Twins

The icy wind howled outside the hospital, slamming against the windows with a ferocity that felt almost unnatural. Winter in Winnipeg was unforgiving, its cold slicing through even the thickest of coats. But Grace's pain was fiercer still.

She gripped Samuel's hand, her fingers digging into his flesh as another wave of contractions tore through her body. Sweat beaded on her brow despite the chill in the air, her breathing shallow and ragged.
"Hold on, Grace," Samuel urged, his voice trembling with equal parts fear and anticipation. "Just a little longer. God is with us."

"Yes," Grace panted, her eyes squeezing shut as the pain reached its peak. "God... is with us."
They had rushed to the hospital in the dead of night, Samuel's taxi weaving through streets blanketed in snow. The drive had been a blur of blaring horns, flashing lights, and Grace's pained groans echoing in his ears.

The hospital itself was a world of sterile white walls and sharp antiseptic scents. Nurses clad in pale blue scrubs hurried them through the maze of corridors, their expressions a mixture of efficiency and mild disinterest.

Grace was admitted quickly, her labor progressing faster than the doctors had expected. Samuel paced the waiting room, his hands clasped together as he murmured prayers under his breath. Fear coiled tightly in his chest, his mind racing with thoughts of all that could go wrong.

He had lost so much already—his status, his security, his dreams of instant success. But Grace was his anchor, her faith the only constant in their turbulent new life. To lose her now would be a devastation he could not endure.

"Mr. Okafor?"

Samuel's head snapped up, his eyes locking onto the nurse who stood before him. She was a short woman with kind eyes and a clipped tone that conveyed urgency.

"Yes?"

"Your wife is asking for you. The babies are coming."

"Babies?" The word tumbled from his mouth in disbelief. "There are two?"

"Yes, Mr. Okafor. Twins."

His legs felt like lead as he followed the nurse into the delivery room. Grace lay on the bed, her face pale but determined. Her eyes found his immediately, relief washing over her as he took her hand.

"Twins," Samuel whispered, his voice cracking. "God has doubled our blessing."

"Or our burden," Grace replied with a weary smile. "But either way, He has chosen to give us both."

The delivery was a blur of shouted instructions, the clatter of instruments, and Grace's strained cries. Samuel's hands shook as he clung to hers, his heart thudding painfully in his chest.

And then, suddenly, there was a cry.

A high-pitched wail filled the room, fierce and demanding. The nurse lifted a tiny, squirming baby into the air, her voice bright with announcement. "It's a boy."

Samuel felt his knees buckle, his body sagging with relief. But before he could fully process the miracle before him, another cry pierced the air.

"It's another boy."

The second baby's cries were softer, more of a whimper than a wail. But his presence was unmistakable—a second life brought forth into the world.

Samuel stared at the infants, his eyes blurred with tears. "Two sons," he whispered, his voice thick with emotion. "Peter and Paul. Just like the apostles."

Grace's exhaustion melted into joy, her smile radiant despite her obvious fatigue. "Yes. Peter and Paul. May they walk with God, always."

The babies were placed into Grace's arms, their tiny bodies swaddled in white blankets. Peter's eyes were tightly shut, his face scrunched into a scowl as he continued to cry. Paul, however, stared up at his mother with wide, curious eyes, his silence both calming and unnerving.

"Already so different," Grace observed, her gaze flickering between the two newborns. "Peter is loud and strong. Paul is quiet and observant."

"They will complement each other," Samuel said, his tone hopeful. "Strength and wisdom."

"God willing."

Samuel pressed his lips to Grace's forehead, his heart swelling with love and gratitude. The road ahead was still fraught with uncertainty, but this moment—this precious, unrepeatable moment—was a victory all its own.

Their sons were born. Their family had grown. And Samuel vowed, with every ounce of resolve he possessed, to give them a future worth living.

Distinct Personalities

Peter and Paul grew quickly, their infancy marked by the predictable rhythms of feeding, crying, and restless nights. Samuel and Grace adjusted to the demands of parenting, their love for their sons deepening with each passing day. But as the years rolled by, it became evident that the twins, though identical in appearance, were remarkably different in nature.

By the time the boys were three years old, their distinct personalities had already begun to shine through. Peter was a whirlwind of energy, his curiosity boundless and his determination relentless. He tore through the apartment like a storm, his little hands reaching for anything within grasp.

"No, Peter! Leave that alone!" Grace would call, her voice equal parts exasperation and affection as she chased after him. But Peter seemed to delight in pushing boundaries, his defiance almost playful.
Paul, in contrast, was quieter, more contemplative. Where Peter dashed headlong into trouble, Paul would sit back and observe, his eyes filled with a curiosity tempered by caution.

He preferred books and toys that required patience—puzzles, blocks, drawings. Grace marveled at the way he could sit for hours, his small fingers fitting pieces together with deliberate precision.

"They are like fire and water," Samuel observed one evening, his voice edged with amusement. "Peter blazes ahead, while Paul flows around obstacles."

"They complement each other," Grace replied, her gaze softening as she watched the twins play. "Just as you said the day they were born."

But their differences were not only a matter of temperament. They were evident even in the way they interacted with others.

Peter craved attention, his enthusiasm drawing people toward him. He would race across the playground, his laughter infectious as he led other children in wild games of tag. Yet, his eagerness often turned to frustration when things did not go his way.

"Peter does not like to be told no," Grace remarked, her voice filled with concern. "He is quick to anger."

"He is strong-willed," Samuel countered. "It can be a blessing if channeled properly."

"But how do we channel it?" Grace wondered aloud, her fingers absently twisting a strand of her hair. "How do we teach him to control himself?"

"With patience and prayer," Samuel replied. "Just as we teach Paul not to be so fearful."

Paul's shyness worried them both. While Peter's confidence sometimes bordered on recklessness, Paul's hesitation often held him back. He clung to Grace's side when visitors came to their apartment, his fingers clutching her skirt like a lifeline.

"He needs time," Grace would say, her tone defensive whenever Samuel raised concerns. "Not everyone is meant to be loud and bold."

But Samuel's worry persisted. He feared that Paul's quiet nature would make him vulnerable, a target for those who preyed on the meek.

"We must teach him to be strong," Samuel insisted. "To speak up for himself. The world is not kind to those who hide in the shadows."

"He is strong in his own way," Grace argued. "He is gentle, yes, but also wise. He sees things that Peter misses."

Their arguments over the boys' development were rare but passionate. Each parent saw something different in their children, their perspectives shaped by their own strengths and weaknesses.

Peter's restlessness grew as he entered his fourth year. He questioned everything—why the sky was blue, why water was wet, why their family went to church every Sunday when other families stayed home.

"Why do we have to pray all the time?" Peter asked one morning, his brow furrowed in genuine confusion.

"Because prayer is how we speak to God," Grace replied, her hands busy folding laundry. "It keeps us connected to Him."

"But I don't hear Him talk back," Peter argued, his tone laced with frustration.

"He speaks in many ways," Grace explained patiently. "Through His word, through our hearts, and through the kindness of others."

Peter's scowl deepened. "I don't understand."

"You will, one day," Grace promised, her voice filled with hope.

Paul, on the other hand, seemed drawn to the teachings of the church. He would sit quietly during the services, his small hands clasped in prayer as his eyes fixed on the pastor with unwavering attention.

"David defeated Goliath because he trusted God," Paul stated one evening, his voice soft but confident. "And I want to be like David."

"You already are," Grace told him, her heart swelling with pride. "You have faith, and that is the greatest strength of all."
Peter, overhearing the conversation, snorted. "I want to be like Goliath. He was stronger."
Grace frowned, her lips tightening. "But strength without wisdom is foolishness."

"I am strong and smart," Peter declared, puffing out his chest. "Smarter than Paul."
Paul did not respond. He simply continued to draw with his crayons, his attention fixed on the picture he was creating.
But Grace saw the hurt in his eyes, the quiet disappointment that his brother's words had inflicted.
It was then that Grace began to worry. Not only about their individual traits, but about the growing tension between them. They were still so young, their paths only just beginning to form. But the seeds of difference had been planted, and Grace feared what those seeds might one day produce.

Samuel remained optimistic, insisting that their differences were strengths meant to complement one another. But Grace could not shake the feeling that the very qualities that made them unique were also pushing them apart.

"God will guide them," she whispered to herself each night, her prayers heavy with the weight of a mother's worry. "He must."

Prayers, Storytelling, and Foundational Values

Despite the struggles of assimilation and the relentless grind of low-wage work, Samuel and Grace sought to build a strong foundation for their children. Their home, however humble, was filled with love, discipline, and unwavering faith.

Every morning before dawn, Samuel would rise from the thin mattress he and Grace shared and kneel beside their bed to pray. His whispered words filled the room like incense, his petitions a plea for strength and guidance.

"Lord, I thank You for another day," Samuel would say, his voice thick with fatigue but strong in faith. "Help me to be a good father. Give me the wisdom to guide my children in Your ways. Protect them, Lord, from the dangers of this world."

Grace would join him moments later, her hands clasped over his. Together, they would pray for their sons, for provision, for guidance. It was their ritual, their daily offering.

By the time Peter and Paul awoke, the aroma of Grace's cooking would fill the apartment. Their breakfast was usually simple—oats, bread, or rice with eggs. But Grace infused every meal with warmth and prayer.

"Eat, my sons," she would say as she placed their plates before them. "And do not forget to thank God for His blessings."

Paul would always bow his head obediently, his small hands clasped as he murmured a prayer of gratitude. Peter, however, often ate first and prayed after—if he prayed at all.

"Why do I have to pray every time?" Peter asked one morning, his voice thick with irritation. "It's just food."

"It is not just food," Grace replied gently. "It is God's provision. We must always give thanks."

Peter rolled his eyes but complied, muttering a quick, half-hearted prayer before digging into his food.

After breakfast, Grace would gather the boys in the living room for their morning devotion. It was a practice she had inherited from her own mother, one she intended to pass down to her sons.

"The Word of God is life," she would tell them, her voice filled with conviction. "It will guide you, protect you, and give you wisdom."

They would read passages from the Bible, Grace's voice steady as she explained their meaning. Paul absorbed every word with wide-eyed fascination, his questions thoughtful and sincere.

"Why did David fight Goliath when he was so small?" Paul asked one morning, his eyes alight with curiosity.

"Because he had faith," Grace replied. "He knew that God was with him. Size does not matter when God is on your side."

"I want to be like David," Paul declared, his small chest swelling with determination.

"And you will be," Grace assured him. "As long as you trust in God."

Peter, however, grew restless during their devotionals. His attention would drift, his fingers drumming impatiently against his knees.

"Why do we always have to read the Bible?" Peter asked one day, his tone more challenging than curious.

"Because the Bible is our guide," Samuel replied sternly. "It teaches us how to live a righteous life."

"But other kids don't read the Bible," Peter countered. "They still have fun."
"There is more to life than fun," Samuel snapped, his frustration seeping into his voice. "You must learn discipline."

Peter scowled but said nothing more. His eyes flickered toward Paul, who was listening intently as Grace read from the book of Psalms.

In the evenings, Grace would gather the boys before bedtime for storytelling. But her stories were never mere entertainment; they were lessons woven into tales of heroes and villains, faith and courage.
"Tell us about Joseph again," Paul would plead, his eyes gleaming with excitement.
"Yes, Mama!" Peter echoed, though his enthusiasm was less about the moral of the story and more about the drama.

Grace would recount the tale of Joseph, his betrayal by his brothers, his imprisonment, and eventual rise to power in Egypt. She spoke with passion, her words painting vivid pictures that captivated their imaginations.
"Joseph was faithful even when things went wrong," Grace would conclude. "And because of his faithfulness, God elevated him. Never forget that, my sons."

Paul's eyes would shine with admiration, his young mind already shaping dreams of his own greatness. Peter, however, would often interrupt with questions about the villains.

"But what about the brothers?" Peter would ask. "They were mean, but nothing bad happened to them."

"They suffered for their actions," Grace explained patiently. "Their guilt weighed heavy on their hearts. And forgiveness came only when they repented."

"But they still got food from Joseph," Peter argued. "So being bad wasn't so bad."

Grace frowned, her brows knitting in concern. "You are missing the point, Peter. It is not about what you get, but who you become."

Peter shrugged, his mind already flitting to other thoughts. But Grace's concern lingered. She feared that Peter's fascination with power and strength would overshadow the lessons she tried so hard to instill.

Samuel, too, noticed the difference between their sons. Paul was obedient and thoughtful, his faith growing stronger with each passing day. Peter, however, remained restless, his curiosity often leading him to question rather than believe.

"They will find their way," Samuel assured Grace one night. "We must continue to teach them. The Word of God will not return void."

"I pray you are right," Grace whispered, her voice heavy with worry. "But Peter...he sees the world so differently."

"Perhaps that is his gift," Samuel replied. "Not all children are meant to walk the same path."

Grace nodded, though her concern did not entirely fade. She continued their rituals of prayer and storytelling, her faith the cornerstone of their family's life. But the divergence between Peter and Paul grew with each passing day, and the seeds of difference continued to take root.

Home and Neighborhood

The apartment Samuel and Grace rented was a modest two-bedroom flat on the second floor of a worn-out building situated in the North End of Winnipeg. The area was far from luxurious; it bore the scars of poverty and neglect.

The paint on the building's exterior had long since peeled away, leaving patches of exposed brick that seemed to defy the relentless Canadian winters.

Their home was small, its walls covered with faded beige paint that Grace had tried to brighten with colorful fabrics from Nigeria. The vibrant Ankara cloths draped over their worn-out couch and pinned to the walls brought a touch of familiarity and warmth to an otherwise drab environment. The floors creaked with each step, and the heating system was as temperamental as the weather outside.

"We will make it beautiful," Grace had declared when they first moved in. "Home is not about where you live. It is about what you build."

They had few possessions—just enough furniture to fill the living room and the boys' bedroom. Peter and Paul shared a small bed, their blankets decorated with cartoon characters Grace had picked up from a local thrift store. Their toys were few, but Grace compensated with storytelling and imagination.

The kitchen was cramped, the counters cluttered with the essentials of survival rather than luxury. Grace prepared most of their meals from scratch, using spices and recipes passed down from her mother. The scent of jollof rice, egusi soup, and fried plantains would often waft through the hallway, luring curious neighbors to their door.

Their neighbors were a mixed assortment of immigrants, low-income families, and students scraping by on minimal wages. The sounds of life drifted through the paper-thin walls—crying babies, blaring televisions, arguments muffled by closed doors.

The North End was not known for its safety. Samuel had learned that quickly during his night shifts as a security guard. Fights broke out frequently on the streets below, and police sirens were a common backdrop to their daily lives.

"I do not like this place," Samuel admitted one night, his voice strained with frustration. "It is not safe for the boys."

"It is what we can afford," Grace replied. "And God will protect us."

"But for how long?" Samuel questioned, his eyes filled with worry. "I see the kind of people who walk these streets. I hear their voices at night—arguing, shouting. This is not the life I wanted for our children."

"It is not the place, but what we make of it," Grace insisted. "We will teach them what is right. They will rise above their surroundings."

But Samuel's concerns only grew as Peter and Paul became old enough to venture outside.

The Choices We Make: Seeds of Destiny

The playground behind their building was little more than a fenced-in patch of dying grass and rusted swings.
Broken bottles and discarded needles often littered the ground, remnants of nights Samuel dared not imagine.

Despite the harsh environment, the boys found joy wherever they could. Peter, with his adventurous spirit, would race across the playground with wild abandon, his laughter echoing against the brick walls. Paul preferred to stay closer to home, his gaze often fixed on the world beyond their apartment's small window.

Their neighbors were a varied assortment. There was Mrs. Chang, an elderly Chinese woman who lived on the floor above them and often offered Grace advice about the local markets. She would smile fondly at the boys whenever they passed her door, pressing candies into their palms with a soft pat on their heads.
"I like her," Paul said one afternoon, his voice muffled by the candy in his mouth.
"She's nice," Peter agreed. "But I like Mr. Brown better. He has a dog."

Mr. Brown was a retired schoolteacher who lived two doors down. He had a German Shepherd named Max, who Peter adored. Mr. Brown would sometimes invite the boys over to play with the dog, his wrinkled face creasing with delight at their uninhibited joy.

"It's good for them to make friends," Mr. Brown told Grace one evening. "Even if it's with an old man like me."
"Thank you," Grace replied, her gratitude genuine. "You have been very kind."

But not all their neighbors were as welcoming. There were those who eyed them with suspicion, their faces twisted with prejudice that spoke louder than words. Samuel noticed the stares, the whispers, the thinly veiled disdain from some of the building's older tenants.

"Why do they look at us like that?" Paul asked one day, his brow furrowed with confusion.
"Because we are different," Grace answered, her tone gentle but firm. "But being different is not wrong."
"They're just stupid," Peter declared, his eyes flashing with defiance. "Who cares what they think?"

"Peter!" Grace scolded, her tone sharp. "We must show kindness, even when others do not."
"But why? They don't deserve it."
"Because God calls us to love everyone," Grace replied. "Even those who do not love us."
Peter's scowl deepened, but he did not argue further. Yet, Grace worried that her words had not truly reached him.

As the months went by, the boys grew more accustomed to their environment. They learned the rhythms of their neighborhood—the times to avoid the playground, the routes safest to walk, the people to trust and the ones to avoid.

But the tension between their upbringing and their surroundings was undeniable. Samuel worried that the harshness of their environment would taint his sons, while Grace continued to insist that faith and love could overcome even the darkest of circumstances.

"God is our shelter," she would say whenever Samuel's worries threatened to consume him. "He will keep us safe."
Samuel hoped she was right. But deep down, his doubts festered like an untreated wound.

Integrating into Canadian Society

From the moment Samuel and Grace stepped off the plane in Winnipeg, they were acutely aware of their differences. The air was cold and crisp, a sharp contrast to the humid warmth of Lagos. But the physical discomfort was nothing compared to the cultural dissonance that would follow.

Samuel's first shock came during his job search.
In Nigeria, he had built a respectable career in logistics, his skills and experience honed through years of dedication. But here, his credentials meant little. Employers skimmed through his resume with expressions of polite dismissal, their eyes glazing over the moment they noted his lack of Canadian experience.

"I have been a supervisor," Samuel would say, his voice tight with frustration. "I have managed teams of men, coordinated shipments across borders. I am qualified."

But his words fell on deaf ears. What mattered more, it seemed, was familiarity with Canadian systems, Canadian customs, Canadian etiquette.
"We must adapt," Grace told him, her tone gentle but firm. "We cannot expect them to change for us."

Yet, adapting was easier said than done. The unspoken rules of social interaction felt foreign to Samuel. Conversations with coworkers were often stilted and awkward. Attempts to make friends were met with polite indifference or outright rejection.

"Why do they act as though I am invisible?" Samuel asked one evening, his shoulders slumped with defeat.

"They do not understand us," Grace replied. "But that does not mean we should stop trying."

Grace's own efforts to integrate were rooted in the church. The small Nigerian congregation they attended provided her with a sense of familiarity and acceptance. The hymns, sung with passionate reverence, echoed those she had grown up with. The sermons, laced with references to struggle and perseverance, resonated deeply with her.

But even within the church, there were divisions. Older immigrants who had been in Canada for decades viewed the newcomers with a mix of pity and disdain. Their advice was often laced with condescension.

"You must learn how things work here," one elder told Samuel after service one Sunday. "Canada is not Nigeria. You cannot expect to succeed if you cling to the old ways."

"What are the old ways?" Samuel challenged, his voice sharper than he intended. "Honesty? Hard work? Dedication? Those things are not limited to one country."

"But your approach is different," the elder replied. "Canadians value politeness, humility. They will not respect you if you appear too aggressive."

Samuel bristled at the comment but said nothing more. The underlying message was clear—he needed to conform or risk remaining an outsider.

Grace, however, adapted more easily. Her work as a home care assistant allowed her to interact with Canadians on a personal level. Her patients were mostly elderly, many of whom were starved for companionship. Grace's warmth and gentleness endeared her to them, her accent a curiosity rather than a barrier.

"They love me," Grace reported to Samuel one evening, her eyes bright with satisfaction. "They say I am kind. That I remind them of their daughters and granddaughters."

"It is different for you," Samuel replied, his voice tinged with envy. "You care for people. They see you as harmless."

"That is not fair," Grace protested. "I work just as hard as you do."

"I know," Samuel conceded, his shoulders slumping. "It's just...they see me as a threat. A man taking jobs from their own."

"They do not know your heart," Grace whispered, her hand clasping his. "But God does. And He will make a way."

Their attempts to integrate extended beyond work and church. They enrolled Peter and Paul in a local daycare, hoping the exposure would help the boys adapt to their new environment. It was a decision made with reluctance, as Samuel feared the influence of unfamiliar customs and values.

"Will they forget who they are?" Samuel asked Grace one night, his voice heavy with concern. "Will they become like...them?"

"They are children," Grace replied. "They will absorb everything around them. It is our duty to teach them the right way."

At daycare, Peter thrived. His outgoing nature made it easy for him to make friends, his laughter and enthusiasm drawing other children toward him. Paul, however, struggled. He remained shy and reserved, preferring to sit alone rather than join in the games his peers played.

The cultural differences between their home life and the outside world were evident. While Grace and Samuel spoke Igbo at home, Peter and Paul quickly adapted to English, their accents shifting as they absorbed the sounds of their new surroundings.

"They are losing their roots," Samuel lamented one day, his voice thick with disappointment.

"They are adapting," Grace corrected. "And so must we."

Samuel's resentment grew as he continued to struggle for acceptance. The casual racism he encountered in the workplace, the subtle slights, the unspoken prejudices—all of it chipped away at his sense of self-worth.

Grace, however, remained resolute. She attended language classes to improve her accent, read books about Canadian history and culture, and made efforts to befriend their neighbors.

"It is not enough to survive," Grace said one night as she prepared dinner. "We must learn to thrive."

"How?" Samuel challenged, his frustration simmering beneath the surface. "How do we thrive when we are treated as less than human?"

"By showing them that we are more," Grace replied. "By rising above their expectations."

Samuel wanted to believe her. He wanted to believe that hard work and faith could overcome the barriers that surrounded them. But the weight of his struggle was growing heavier with each passing day. Yet, through it all, Grace's faith remained unshaken. She continued to build bridges where Samuel saw only walls, her determination a quiet but powerful force.

"God will make a way," she would say whenever Samuel's anger threatened to consume him. "He has not brought us this far to abandon us."

Samuel tried to hold on to her words, but doubt had already begun to creep into his heart.

Challenges

The path Samuel and Grace walked was riddled with obstacles. Their journey to Canada had been driven by hope, but the reality of their new life was far from the dream they had envisioned. With each passing day, they were reminded that their status as immigrants came with trials they had not anticipated.

The first challenge was financial instability. The money they had saved before leaving Nigeria was quickly depleted by the high cost of living in Winnipeg. Rent, utilities, groceries, and childcare expenses consumed their meager earnings. Samuel's jobs, which ranged from office cleaning to security work, paid little more than minimum wage. His qualifications meant nothing without Canadian experience or recognition.

"What do they mean by 'Canadian experience'?" Samuel often grumbled, his frustration mounting with every job interview that ended in rejection.
"I have worked for years, managing logistics for a major company. But here, they act as if I am a child who knows nothing."

Grace tried to comfort him, her words laced with the faith that had carried them this far. "They do not know your worth, Samuel. But God does. We must be patient."
But patience was a hard virtue to practice when bills loomed and opportunities dwindled. Samuel took on as many shifts as he could, his body weary from long hours and relentless labor. His dignity suffered blow after blow, but his resolve remained intact.

Grace's job as a home care assistant was equally demanding. Her patients were often elderly and frail, requiring constant attention. The physical strain of lifting and bathing them left her muscles aching, but she endured with a gentleness that earned her the affection of her clients.

"You are so kind," one of her patients, Mrs. Patterson, had told her. "You remind me of my own daughter. Always so gentle."

Grace smiled at the compliment, but there were days when her smile felt forced, her energy depleted. She worked double shifts when necessary, her own health often neglected in the pursuit of financial stability.

Their financial struggles were compounded by the harshness of the Canadian winters. The cold seeped into their bones, a relentless adversary they were never truly prepared for. Samuel's jobs often required him to stand outside in frigid temperatures, his fingers numb despite the gloves he wore.

"We must buy proper clothing," Grace insisted one evening, her arms wrapped around herself as she shivered beneath their thin blankets.

"With what money?" Samuel snapped, his frustration bleeding into his tone.

"We will find a way," Grace replied, her voice steady. "God will provide."

Another challenge they faced was cultural dissonance. The values they had grown up with—respect for elders, communal living, faithfulness to traditions—seemed almost alien in their new environment. Their neighbors were polite, but distant. Attempts to form friendships were often met with courteous smiles that never reached the eyes.
"They are kind," Grace would say. "But they do not understand us."

Samuel grew bitter as he continued to encounter discrimination, both subtle and blatant.
Employers who claimed to value diversity but overlooked his applications. Customers who eyed him with suspicion during his security shifts. Neighbors who offered polite greetings but nothing more.
"I am tired of being treated like an outsider," Samuel admitted one night, his voice raw with anger. "No matter how hard I work, it is never enough."
"It is enough for us," Grace whispered. "You are enough for us."

But Samuel's frustrations only grew. His pride, once strong and unshakeable, had been worn down by years of rejection and dismissal. He feared that he would never truly belong in this foreign land.

Even within their church, divisions persisted. Some of the older immigrants who had settled in Canada decades earlier looked down on Samuel and Grace, offering unsolicited advice with condescension rather than compassion.

"You must learn to be more like them," one elder told Samuel. "Your accent is too strong. Your mannerisms are too blunt. Canadians do not like that."
"Why must I change myself to be accepted?" Samuel countered, his frustration bubbling over.
"Because if you do not, you will remain at the bottom."

Samuel hated those words. Hated the idea that success required him to shed parts of himself. But deep down, he feared there was truth in the elder's harsh advice.

Raising their children in such an environment was another challenge. Samuel and Grace were determined to teach Peter and Paul their own values, but the outside world often clashed with their efforts.
At daycare, Peter thrived. His outgoing nature earned him friends quickly, but his teachers complained of his stubbornness and refusal to follow rules.

"Peter is very bright," one teacher told Grace. "But he challenges authority too often."

"What does that mean?" Grace asked, her brow creased with worry.

"It means he does not listen. He questions everything. That can be a strength, but it can also be a problem if he doesn't learn to conform."

Grace bristled at the word "conform." She wanted her children to be confident, not subdued.

Paul's challenges were of a different nature. His shyness made him an easy target for teasing, and his reluctance to speak up often left him isolated.

"He doesn't join in with the other children," another teacher noted. "He seems afraid."

"He is not afraid," Grace replied, her voice laced with defensiveness. "He is thoughtful. He takes his time."

The constant criticisms weighed heavily on Grace's heart. She feared that their efforts to protect their sons from the harshness of their surroundings were not enough.

Samuel, meanwhile, grew increasingly bitter. His resentment toward the society that had rejected him spilled over into his interactions with his children. He was harsh with Peter, demanding obedience and respect. He was stern with Paul, pushing him to be braver, stronger.

"We cannot coddle them," Samuel insisted. "The world will not be kind to them. They must be prepared."

But Grace feared that Samuel's strictness would drive their sons away rather than prepare them for the challenges ahead.

And through it all, their faith remained both a comfort and a test. It was easy to trust God when the path was smooth. But now, with every step fraught with hardship, they struggled to maintain the hope that had once carried them across the ocean.

Chapter Two:

Footsteps in a New Land

From Toddlerhood to Elementary School

The early years of Peter and Paul's lives were spent within the cocoon of their parents' teachings and traditions. But as they grew from toddlers into young boys, their world expanded beyond the small apartment in Winnipeg's North End. The time had come for them to leave the familiar safety of home and step into the larger world of elementary school.

Samuel and Grace had enrolled them in a local public school, hoping that the exposure to new ideas and experiences would help their sons adapt to the Canadian way of life. But the decision had not been made lightly.

"What if they lose who they are?" Samuel had questioned one evening, his brow furrowed with concern. "What if they forget their roots?"

"They will not forget," Grace assured him. "We are their parents. We will teach them who they are. But they must learn to live in this world, as well."

The school was a large, brick building with colorful murals painted along its walls. Children of various backgrounds and cultures crowded the playground, their laughter and chatter a constant hum of life. For Peter and Paul, it was both thrilling and terrifying. Peter thrived almost immediately.

His boundless energy and natural charisma drew other children to him like moths to a flame. Within days, he had established himself as a leader among his peers, his loud voice often rising above the rest during games and group activities.

"Peter is a natural leader," his teacher noted during a parent-teacher conference. "But he can be stubborn. He doesn't like to follow instructions if they don't make sense to him."

"That sounds like Peter," Grace said with a smile that was both proud and concerned. "He always questions everything."

"He's bright," the teacher continued. "But he's also easily frustrated. When things don't go his way, he can be...challenging."

"We will speak with him," Samuel promised, though his tone lacked conviction. He admired Peter's assertiveness, even if it sometimes bordered on defiance.

Paul's experience, however, was markedly different. Where Peter thrived, Paul struggled. The noise and activity of the school overwhelmed him. He clung to Grace's hand on that first day, his small body trembling with nerves.

"You'll be fine," Grace assured him, kneeling to meet his gaze. "God is with you, Paul. Always."

Paul nodded but said nothing. His eyes remained fixed on the floor as Grace gently pried his fingers from her hand and guided him toward the classroom.

At school, Paul remained quiet and reserved. He avoided the noisy games Peter enjoyed, preferring instead to sit by himself during recess. His teachers noted his intelligence but expressed concern about his reluctance to participate.
"Paul is very bright," one teacher told Grace during a meeting. "But he doesn't speak up. He's always in the background, observing rather than engaging."
"He is thoughtful," Grace replied defensively. "He likes to understand before he acts."

"But if he doesn't learn to interact with others, he may fall behind socially," the teacher insisted. "It's something you should work on at home."
The words stung Grace's heart like a rebuke. She wanted her sons to excel, but not at the expense of their identity.

Peter and Paul's divergent experiences at school became more pronounced with each passing year. While Peter accumulated friends with ease, Paul remained an outsider, his shyness often mistaken for aloofness.

Their differences even extended to their schoolwork. Peter excelled at subjects that required creativity and spontaneity. Art, physical education, and drama were his strongholds. But he struggled with tasks that required patience and discipline.

Paul, on the other hand, excelled in reading and writing. His reports were meticulous, his essays filled with insight beyond his years. But his reluctance to speak up during class discussions often left him overlooked.

Samuel and Grace tried their best to support both boys, though their methods differed. Samuel admired Peter's boldness and sought to encourage his assertive nature.

"You must be strong," Samuel would tell Peter, his voice thick with pride. "The world belongs to those who seize it."

Grace, however, worried that Peter's brashness would lead him down a reckless path. She encouraged him to be kind, to temper his strength with compassion.

"Power without wisdom is dangerous," Grace would remind him. "You must listen as well as speak."

With Paul, Samuel was sterner. He worried that his quiet nature would leave him vulnerable to a world that often rewarded aggression over thoughtfulness. "You must speak up, Paul," Samuel would insist. "You cannot hide in the shadows. The world will pass you by if you do."

But Grace saw something special in Paul's gentleness. She encouraged him to embrace his introspective nature, to trust that his quiet strength was not a weakness.
"God has made you the way you are for a reason," Grace would say, her voice tender. "You do not need to be like Peter. You only need to be yourself."

But Paul's struggles persisted. He often returned home from school with his shoulders slumped, his eyes heavy with disappointment. Grace would comfort him as best she could, but the seeds of insecurity were already taking root.
"Why can't I be like Peter?" Paul asked one night, his voice small and broken.

"Because you are Paul," Grace replied, pulling him into her arms. "And that is more than enough."

Samuel watched their sons with growing concern. Their differences were becoming more apparent with each passing day. While Peter's confidence flourished, Paul's quiet nature seemed to hold him back.

"They are like night and day," Samuel told Grace one evening. "I fear for them both."
"They will find their way," Grace insisted. "We must only continue to guide them."
But Samuel's doubts remained. He feared that their struggles at school were only the beginning of greater challenges to come.

Making Friends, Adapting to a New Culture, and Facing Subtle Discrimination

School was a microcosm of the world Samuel and Grace had brought their children into. It was a place of learning, yes, but also of harsh lessons that went beyond the classroom. For Peter and Paul, it was their first real exposure to the complexities of fitting in.

Peter, with his boundless energy and fearless curiosity, adapted quickly. His enthusiasm drew other children to him, and before long, he had established himself as a popular figure among his classmates.

His boldness made him a leader, someone other children admired for his daring.

During recess, Peter would organize games of soccer or tag, his loud, clear voice barking orders that others were quick to follow. His confidence made him magnetic. But that same confidence often bordered on arrogance.

"He's doing well," Grace noted proudly during a parent-teacher meeting. "He seems to have made many friends."
"Yes," Peter's teacher agreed. "He's very social and has a natural charisma. But..."
"But?" Grace echoed, her smile faltering.
"He can be... abrasive. He's quick to challenge authority if he doesn't agree with something. It's good that he's assertive, but sometimes he can come off as disrespectful."
Grace's brows furrowed with concern. "We will speak to him."

But Samuel saw something admirable in Peter's defiance. It was a trait he had come to rely on himself—standing firm in the face of injustice and prejudice. Yet, he feared that Peter's boldness, if not tempered, would lead to trouble.

Paul's experience was markedly different. The noise and activity of the playground overwhelmed him. While Peter thrived in the chaos, Paul retreated into himself, his small frame often hunched as he watched other children from a distance.

"He's shy," Grace admitted to Samuel one evening. "But that's just who he is."

"It is more than shyness," Samuel countered, his voice lined with frustration. "He is afraid. He needs to be stronger."

Paul's difficulties were not limited to social interactions. While Peter's exuberance made him a leader among his peers, Paul's quietness left him vulnerable. Other children noticed his reluctance to speak up, and some began to exploit that weakness.

"Why doesn't your brother ever talk?" one boy sneered one afternoon, his voice loud enough for others to hear. "Is he stupid or something?"

Peter, overhearing the taunt, bristled with anger. "Shut up!" he snapped, his fists clenched. "Paul is smarter than all of you."

"Oh yeah?" the boy shot back. "Then why doesn't he ever say anything?"

Peter's response was swift and physical. His punch landed squarely on the boy's shoulder, drawing gasps from those around them.

"Peter! No!" Paul cried, his eyes wide with horror. "You're not supposed to hit people."

"But he was making fun of you," Peter argued, his chest heaving. "No one does that. Not to my brother."

The incident earned Peter a reprimand from his teacher and a stern lecture from Samuel. But it also deepened the bond between the brothers, albeit in a way Grace found troubling.
"They are relying on each other too much," Grace worried aloud one night. "Peter is trying to protect Paul, but he's doing it the wrong way."
"Peter is strong," Samuel replied. "But Paul must learn to stand up for himself."

Beyond their interactions with other children, Peter and Paul also grappled with the challenge of adapting to a culture that often felt foreign. The expectations placed upon them by their parents sometimes clashed with what they experienced at school.

"Why do we have to pray all the time?" Peter asked one evening, his voice thick with frustration. "No one else does. They all get to have fun."
"Because we are not like everyone else," Samuel answered firmly. "We have values. We have God."
"But what if I just want to be like them?" Peter muttered, his eyes downcast.

Paul, too, felt the weight of being different. His classmates would make fun of his name, his accent, the food he brought for lunch. They would wrinkle their noses and ask, "What's that smell?" or snicker when he struggled to pronounce certain words.

"It's not fair," Paul whispered one day, his head bowed as Grace wiped tears from his cheeks. "Why do they hate me?"

"They do not hate you," Grace assured him, her voice thick with compassion. "They simply do not understand. And sometimes, people mock what they do not understand."

"But I want them to understand," Paul pleaded. "I want to be like them."

"No," Grace said softly but firmly. "You must be who God made you to be. You are special, Paul. Never forget that."

The boys' differences in adapting to their new environment only grew more apparent as they progressed through school. Peter's assertiveness earned him friendships, but it also made him a target for teachers who viewed his boldness as disrespect. Paul's quiet nature kept him out of trouble, but it also kept him isolated.

Despite the challenges, Grace and Samuel continued to encourage their sons to excel. They pushed Peter to channel his energy productively and urged Paul to find his voice.

But as the years passed, the boys began to drift further apart. Peter grew bolder, his desire to fit in leading him to seek approval from friends who did not share his parents' values. Paul, meanwhile, retreated deeper into himself, finding solace in books and the rare moments of kindness he encountered.

The seeds of divergence had been planted, and neither Samuel nor Grace could foresee the harvest that would one day come.

Academic Performance and Parental Expectations

Samuel and Grace had always placed a high value on education. To them, it was not only the key to opportunity but a sacred responsibility—an inheritance they intended to pass down. In Nigeria, academic excellence had been revered, almost as a form of worship. In Canada, they hoped it would be their sons' bridge to belonging and success.

"Education is your ladder," Samuel would often say. "Climb it, and you rise. Neglect it, and you fall."

Peter and Paul, however, responded to their parents' expectations in very different ways.

The Choices We Make: Seeds of Destiny

From the beginning, Paul displayed a quiet but remarkable aptitude for learning. He excelled in reading and writing, often finishing assignments ahead of his classmates. His handwriting was neat, his answers thoughtful and precise. Teachers frequently praised his diligence, though they often noted his lack of participation in group discussions. "Paul is very bright," one teacher reported during a conference. "But he prefers to work alone. He doesn't speak up much, which sometimes affects his marks in oral presentations."

Grace nodded, her face glowing with pride. "He has always been a deep thinker. He will speak when he is ready."

At home, Paul devoured books. While Peter played outside or fiddled with gadgets, Paul would sit in a corner with a novel, his eyes scanning each page with a hunger for knowledge. He asked complex questions—about God, about the world, about people. Grace encouraged his curiosity, seeing in him a reflection of her own love for learning.

Peter's academic journey, on the other hand, was turbulent. He was smart—no one doubted that—but his intelligence came with resistance.

He challenged teachers, questioned rules, and rarely followed instructions to the letter.

While he performed well in subjects like art, physical education, and drama, his grades in math, science, and language arts fluctuated.

"Peter has potential," said his third-grade teacher. "But he doesn't apply himself. He rushes through tests, refuses to revise, and often distracts others."
Samuel's face darkened. "He is smart. He just doesn't like being told what to do."
"That's part of the problem," the teacher replied. "We need to help him understand that discipline is part of growth."

Samuel took the comment personally. He had raised his sons to respect authority, to understand the value of effort. To hear that Peter lacked discipline was like hearing that he himself had failed.
At home, Peter bristled under his father's expectations.
"Why do you always compare me to Paul?" he shouted one evening after a particularly tense exchange.
"Because Paul does his work!" Samuel snapped. "He takes school seriously. You—you act as if life is a game!"
"I'm not Paul!" Peter yelled. "I don't want to be like him!"

The silence that followed was heavy. Grace stepped in, her voice firm but gentle. "No one is asking you to be Paul, Peter. But you must try. You must give your best."

Peter's eyes shimmered with frustration. "My best isn't good enough for Dad."

Samuel said nothing. He turned away, the sting of his son's words settling deep in his chest.

Grace worked hard to balance her encouragement between both boys. She celebrated Paul's academic achievements with quiet praise and tried to affirm Peter's strengths in creativity and leadership.

"You are both gifted," she would say at dinner. "But in different ways. God does not make mistakes."

Yet the comparisons were inevitable. Report cards became a source of tension. Paul's consistent A's and teacher comments about his diligence were met with proud smiles. Peter's C's and D's triggered lectures and restrictions.

"I don't know what to do with him," Samuel confessed one night as he sat with Grace. "I try to be firm, but the more I push, the more he pulls away."

"Maybe he needs a different approach," Grace suggested. "He's not like you, Samuel. He needs to be led, not pushed."

"I don't want him to fail," Samuel whispered. "I want him to succeed. To be better than me."
"He won't fail," Grace said softly. "He just has a different path. But he will find his way."

Still, Samuel struggled to let go of the rigid expectations he had brought with him from Nigeria. In his eyes, academic success was non-negotiable. He feared that anything less would doom his children to the same struggle he had fought so hard to escape.
Peter, sensing his father's disappointment, began to hide his struggles. He stopped showing his test papers. He pretended to have no homework. He smiled even as his grades slipped.

Paul, meanwhile, carried the burden of being the "good son." His quiet success came with the pressure to always excel, always perform.
"I got an A," he said quietly one evening, placing his report card on the table.
Grace beamed. Samuel nodded, though his gaze lingered on Peter, who stared down at his untouched plate.
"Why don't you ever ask me about my grades?" Peter asked suddenly.
Samuel looked up, caught off guard. "Do you have something to show?"

Peter's silence was answer enough.

Grace reached across the table, placing her hand over Peter's. "We care about both of you. We want you to do your best—not just for us, but for yourself."

Peter's eyes met hers, a mixture of anger and hurt swirling in his gaze. "I don't think my best will ever be enough."

Grace said nothing. Instead, she pulled him into a hug, her heart aching with the weight of the expectations that were slowly pulling her family apart.

Peer Influences and Early Signs of Divergence in Interests

By the time Peter and Paul reached the fourth grade, their lives had begun to move in distinctly different directions. Though they shared a room, a school, and parents who loved them deeply, the forces shaping them from outside the home began to steer them down separate paths.

Peter's magnetic personality continued to draw friends to him.

But increasingly, those friends came from groups that Grace and Samuel viewed with growing concern. Boys who talked back to teachers, who skipped class, who seemed to revel in testing boundaries. They were adventurous, daring—and careless.

"Peter is spending too much time with those boys from across the street," Grace said one afternoon as she watched her son skateboarding on the cracked pavement. "They are always in trouble."
Samuel grunted in agreement, his eyes following the group with a cautious gaze. "He thinks they're bold. He doesn't see the danger in being reckless."

At first, the influence seemed harmless. Peter began picking up slang phrases and mimicking the bravado of older boys. He laughed louder, interrupted more often, and became more dismissive when corrected at home.
"It's just a phase," Grace hoped. "He's trying to fit in."

But it wasn't just mimicry. Peter was genuinely drawn to their way of life—the thrill of breaking minor rules, the camaraderie of rebellion. He loved being the center of attention, the leader of the pack, the boy others looked to when something exciting—or dangerous—was about to happen.

Paul, by contrast, sought refuge in quieter places. His circle of friends was small, mostly children who shared his love for books, drawing, or quiet games. He avoided conflict, detested loud confrontations, and often spent recess alone when his friends were absent.

"I like it when it's quiet," Paul explained to Grace one day. "I can think better."

Samuel worried about Paul's withdrawal. "He's too soft," he said. "The world isn't kind to boys like that."

"He's not soft," Grace countered. "He's sensitive. There's a difference."

But Samuel remained uneasy. While Peter was beginning to emulate strength in the wrong ways, Paul seemed to retreat further into his shell.

The boys' interests began to diverge more clearly with time. Peter grew fascinated with sports—especially soccer and basketball. He spent hours practicing outside, often dragging other boys from the neighborhood to join him. He loved the noise, the motion, the adrenaline. Winning excited him, and even losing seemed to fire him up for the next challenge.

"Maybe sports will give him direction," Samuel mused one evening. "He needs structure. Competition might help."

Grace was less certain. "He loves it, yes. But sometimes he comes home angry when things don't go his way. He's too emotional about it."

Paul's world was different. He had developed an interest in science and storytelling. He wrote short poems and made lists of facts about planets, insects, and biblical heroes. He once wrote an illustrated story about David and Goliath from the perspective of David's sling.

"Paul has a gift," Grace said, showing Samuel the story. "He sees things from a different angle. He might be a writer one day."

Samuel nodded slowly. "As long as he doesn't forget to speak up for himself."

Though their bond as twins remained, Peter and Paul now occupied two different worlds. Their conversations became less frequent. Peter teased Paul about his "nerdy" interests, while Paul rolled his eyes at Peter's obsession with popularity.

"Come play soccer with us," Peter called out one afternoon.

"I'm working on my science project," Paul replied.

"You're always doing that boring stuff," Peter scoffed. "Come on. You need to get out sometimes."

"It's not boring to me," Paul said quietly, turning back to his book.

Their differences spilled over into how they responded to peer pressure. Peter, eager to impress, was increasingly willing to compromise his values to fit in. He lied about homework, took credit for others' work, and once even shoplifted a candy bar to prove his courage.

When Grace found out, she was devastated.
"Why would you do such a thing?" she asked, hurt brimming in her eyes.

Peter shrugged. "Everyone does it. It's no big deal."
"It is a big deal!" Samuel thundered. "In this house, we do not lie. We do not steal."
Peter's jaw tightened. "Maybe in this house. But out there, it's different."

Paul, overhearing the conversation, said nothing. But that night, he wrote in his notebook: *Right is right, even if no one is doing it. Wrong is wrong, even if everyone is.*

As the gap between them widened, Samuel and Grace struggled to keep them aligned. They continued to pray, to teach, to guide. But the external influences were strong. And the boys, though bound by blood, were now shaped by vastly different forces.

The Choices We Make: Seeds of Destiny

Grace's Involvement in the Church and Introducing the Boys to Christian Teachings

For Grace, the church was more than a building—it was her sanctuary, her family, her foundation. It was in the sanctuary's quiet stillness, beneath stained glass windows and the soft hum of worship music, that she felt most at home in a foreign land. In Winnipeg, where everything else felt unfamiliar, the church was the only place that mirrored the rhythms of her life back in Nigeria.

From the moment they arrived in Canada, Grace had made it a priority to find a congregation where she could continue to serve God and surround her family with a faith-filled community. They settled into a modest Nigerian church located in a converted hall on the edge of their neighborhood. It was not grand, but it was vibrant—filled with the sounds of drums, clapping, choruses, and prayers that rose with fervent passion.

Grace immediately immersed herself in the church's activities. She joined the women's fellowship, taught in the children's ministry, and volunteered for cleaning and hospitality duties. Her presence became a source of comfort and leadership. People began calling her "Sister Grace," a title that reflected the quiet dignity and devotion she carried.

"This church reminds me of home," she told Samuel one Sunday afternoon. "It is where I gather strength. And our boys need to grow up in this strength."

Samuel respected her commitment, even if he didn't share the same emotional attachment. He attended regularly but remained somewhat reserved, his mind often preoccupied with work and the pressures of providing.

Grace, however, made the church a central part of their family's life. Sunday mornings were sacred. The family would wake early, dress in their best clothes, and walk to the church together, often reciting memory verses along the way.

"Thy word is a lamp unto my feet, and a light unto my path," Grace would say.

"Amen," Paul would whisper, his little voice sincere.

Peter, always one to challenge, would often mumble the verses half-heartedly or ask, "Why do we have to memorize all these? Does God need us to quote them back to Him?"

"God's Word is not for Him to hear," Grace would explain patiently. "It's for you to live by."

At church, Peter and Paul attended children's classes where they were taught Bible stories, sang songs, and participated in skits during special programs.

Paul loved the stories—especially those of David, Joseph, and Daniel. He listened intently, asked deep questions, and often repeated lessons at home.
"Mama," he once asked, "Why did Joseph forgive his brothers after all they did?"
"Because God calls us to forgive," Grace answered, looking into his eyes. "And because love is stronger than revenge."

Peter, on the other hand, found the stories amusing but not particularly meaningful. He enjoyed the dramatizations and songs but questioned the application.
"So, David beat a giant with a stone," he once said. "Cool story, but it's not like we fight giants anymore."
"You fight different kinds of giants," Grace replied. "Pride, fear, anger, temptation—these are giants too."

Still, Grace was determined not to force the faith upon them but to nurture it through love, prayer, and consistent teaching. She made it a daily practice to read a devotional with the boys each morning before school. She taught them to pray, not just in repetition but from the heart.
"Talk to God like He is your friend," she would say. "Tell Him your worries, your hopes, your thanks."

The Choices We Make: Seeds of Destiny

Paul took this to heart. He began keeping a small prayer journal, where he scribbled down short prayers in uneven handwriting.

"Dear God, help me to be strong. Help me to make good friends. Help me to understand Your Word."

Peter prayed too—but more out of habit than conviction. Sometimes he would rush through the words, eager to return to whatever game or activity he had been interrupted from.

One evening, after a powerful sermon on obedience and faith, Grace sat her sons down.

"Boys, you must choose now what kind of men you want to become. God has given you both different gifts, but your heart is what He truly desires."

Paul nodded solemnly. Peter shrugged. "I'm still figuring that out," he said.

"That's okay," Grace responded. "But don't wait too long. This world will try to shape you if you do not let God shape you first."

Grace's consistency in prayer and teaching slowly bore fruit in Paul's life. He developed a genuine reverence for God. He read the Bible on his own and often tried to apply its principles in his day-to-day actions. He reminded Peter to pray before meals, corrected him when he spoke harshly, and sometimes defended other children who were bullied.

Peter, though respectful of his mother, remained detached. He believed in God—but more in concept than in commitment. His faith was passive, a background soundtrack to his louder, more dominant pursuits.

Grace often knelt in her room at night, tears running down her face as she prayed for her sons.
"Lord, let them not depart from Your ways. Give me wisdom to guide them. Touch Peter's heart. Deepen Paul's walk with You. And help me not to grow weary in this calling."

Church was her anchor. And through its routines and rituals, she sowed seeds of faith in the hearts of her sons, trusting that in time, God would bring the increase.

Community Events and Cultural Gatherings

Amidst the daily grind of work, school, and church, community events and cultural gatherings became a vital source of beauty in Samuel and Grace's life in Canada. These gatherings offered a rare opportunity to reconnect with their roots, share stories, and pass on the customs they held dear to their children.

The Nigerian Association of Manitoba, a local group formed by Nigerian immigrants, hosted regular events to bring together families from across the province. From Independence Day celebrations to cultural food fairs and town hall meetings, these occasions provided a comforting sense of familiarity and solidarity.

"It feels like home," Grace would often say, smiling as she watched women dressed in colorful ankara and gele swap recipes and testimonies while children darted through crowds of dancing adults.

The twins had different reactions to these events. Paul was drawn to the storytelling and the traditional drumming. He enjoyed listening to elders recount tales from their villages—stories of bravery, honesty, and divine intervention. He asked questions, listened attentively, and even began to show interest in learning Igbo, his parents' native language.

Peter, on the other hand, was more interested in the food and the games. He loved the jollof rice, suya, puff-puff, and chin chin that lined the buffet tables. He participated in soccer tournaments and races but often grew impatient during the more reflective parts of the events.

"Why do we have to sit through all the speeches?" he asked one afternoon, balancing a plate heaped with food.

"Because it is important to know who we are and where we come from," Grace answered. "These stories are your inheritance."

Peter shrugged. "All I know is I'm Canadian. That's what everyone else sees."

Samuel overheard the remark and pulled Peter aside. "Never forget your roots. Canada is where you live, but Nigeria is your heritage. You must carry it with pride."

Some weekends, the family would attend African gospel concerts and talent shows hosted by neighboring churches. Grace would often volunteer in planning committees, organizing choir presentations and cultural fashion showcases. Her voice became known in many circles—not just for her singing but for her wisdom and quiet leadership. Paul occasionally performed Bible memory verses during children's segments, his voice shy but clear. Grace beamed each time, mouthing the words alongside him.

Peter, though less interested in performing, enjoyed the communal energy. He thrived on the social atmosphere and sought out other boys his age. He developed friendships that extended beyond school—some positive, others that began to echo the same worrisome patterns Grace and Samuel had already seen.

During the summer, the community held a family picnic at a local park, where families brought food, music, and games. Samuel helped with setting up the grills and tents, while Grace led a women's prayer group under a gazebo.

"You do so much," one woman commented to Grace. "Why not let others carry the load for once?" Grace smiled. "This is our new village. We must build it with our hands, our hearts, and our prayers." For Samuel, the gatherings were a welcome break from his exhausting work schedule. He found joy in reconnecting with old friends, laughing over shared memories, and speaking in his native tongue without the strain of explanation. It was a rare space where he felt seen and valued.

Yet even in these gatherings, the cracks in his relationship with Peter became more apparent. When elders gathered to bless the children, Peter often looked away, uninterested in the prayers or proverbs.
"You must learn to receive wisdom," Samuel once scolded after an event. "These people have walked roads you have yet to see."
"I don't need their blessings," Peter muttered. "I just want to live my own life."

Samuel was wounded by his son's words, but Grace remained hopeful.

"He is still learning," she said quietly. "Keep sowing seeds. God will give the increase."

Despite the occasional tensions, the cultural gatherings remained an anchor for their family. They provided a rhythm, a sense of celebration amid struggle, and a living connection to a heritage that might otherwise fade in the Canadian winter.

Paul began journaling after each event, writing about the food, the stories, and the things he learned. "I want to remember everything," he told his mother. "So I can teach my children one day."

Grace's heart swelled with gratitude. In a world that constantly pushed assimilation, her family was fighting—sometimes stumbling, but always striving—to hold on to their faith, their values, and their identity.

The Twins' Differing Reactions to Church and Community Activities

Though Peter and Paul shared the same home, attended the same church, and participated in the same community gatherings, their individual responses to these experiences were worlds apart.

As they grew, so did the divergence in how each brother connected—or disconnected—from the spiritual and cultural life Grace and Samuel so diligently cultivated.

Paul embraced church life with a quiet, sincere devotion. He found comfort in the routine: Sunday school classes, scripture recitations, youth prayer meetings, and family devotionals. The stories of David's courage, Joseph's integrity, and Daniel's faithfulness weren't just bedtime tales to him—they were guiding lights.

"I want to be like Daniel," Paul told Grace one day after church, his voice calm and resolved. "He prayed even when the law said not to."
Grace smiled, placing a gentle hand on his shoulder. "Then be bold like Daniel. Always stand for what is right."
Paul often volunteered during children's presentations, reciting memory verses and even offering short prayers at the pulpit during youth events.
His teachers admired his attentiveness and his ability to recall Bible stories with accuracy and depth.

"Your son is a blessing," the Sunday school coordinator once told Grace. "He listens, he learns, and he has a good heart."

Peter, however, was a different story. While he respected his parents' faith, he found the predictability of church activities boring and unnecessary. To him, the hymns were too slow, the sermons too long, and the teachings too abstract.

"Why do we have to go every Sunday?" he asked one morning, groaning as Grace laid out his church clothes. "It's the same thing every week."
"It's not about entertainment," Grace replied. "It's about growth. The Word of God is like food for your spirit." "I'm not hungry," Peter muttered.

Though he sat through the services, his mind often wandered. He slouched in his seat, fidgeted during prayers, and whispered jokes to friends during sermons.

His Sunday school teachers frequently had to correct him for disrupting class or failing to do his memory work.
"Peter has a strong personality," one of them told Grace with a cautious smile. "He's sharp and outspoken. But he's also... distracted."

Grace and Samuel tried various ways to engage him. They encouraged him to join the youth choir, participate in church dramas, or help with ushering.

The Choices We Make: Seeds of Destiny

At times he would show brief enthusiasm—especially when it involved being on stage—but the interest rarely lasted.

Paul, by contrast, continued to thrive. His favorite part of church was the midweek Bible study. While others—including his peers—found it too intense or long, Paul would sit attentively with a notebook in hand, jotting down verses and questions to ask later at home.

"Why did Jesus say, 'Father, forgive them' while He was on the cross?" Paul once asked his father.

Samuel looked at his son with admiration. "Because He loved even those who hurt Him. That's the kind of heart we must have."

Paul nodded. "I want to be like that."

At community events, the difference between the twins was equally apparent. Paul preferred the cultural storytelling, traditional songs, and testimonies shared by older members. He liked to listen, to learn.

Peter gravitated to the crowd. He wanted to compete in soccer matches, lead dance challenges, and be at the center of youthful energy. When elders began to share advice or prayers, he often tuned out or disappeared to join friends in the parking lot.

"You didn't hear anything that was said," Grace scolded after one event. "There were words of wisdom spoken."
"I was busy having fun," Peter replied. "I already hear enough preaching every week."

Samuel pulled him aside that evening. "Peter, these gatherings are not just about food and fun. They're about identity. About staying grounded."
"I know who I am," Peter shot back. "I don't need all this to figure it out."
"But you are still learning who you are," Samuel replied. "And these things will help you remember where you come from and who you belong to."

While Peter rebelled in subtle ways—dodging responsibilities at church or mocking serious discussions—Paul's faith began to take root. He began helping his mother with Bible study outlines for the children's class. He asked Samuel if he could begin fasting once a week, just to draw closer to God.
"You're still young," Samuel said, surprised. "You don't have to fast yet."
"I want to," Paul replied. "Not for food, but for focus."

Grace looked on in awe. "God is working in his heart."

The Choices We Make: Seeds of Destiny

Peter, meanwhile, grew more distant. He began making excuses to skip church events and started pushing back more aggressively when asked to participate.

"You're not giving him room to discover his own path," Samuel told Grace one evening. "We must guide him, yes, but we must also pray that he finds his way."

Grace nodded solemnly. "But I will never stop speaking truth. Even when he rolls his eyes, I'll keep planting seeds. One day, they will grow."

Despite the tension and contrast, one thing remained: the unwavering love of their parents. And the prayers that filled their home each night, asking God to keep their sons in His care—even as their paths continued to part.

Chapter Three:

Brothers Apart

Pre-Teen Years and Emerging Individuality

The shift from childhood to pre-teenhood was subtle, but unmistakable. It began with changes in tone, in preferences, in the quiet assertion of "I don't like that anymore." And for Peter and Paul, it was the start of something deeper—an emergence of individuality that would define the course of their lives.

Paul grew into his structure. He liked routines, excelled in organized settings, and took joy in responsibilities that seemed mature for his age. He was precise with his words, careful with his time, and naturally drawn to leadership roles—even when he didn't ask for them.

Peter, on the other hand, bloomed with unpredictability. He questioned rules more often, found excitement in the unconventional, and resisted being boxed in. Where Paul thrived on clarity, Peter craved adventure. He wasn't reckless—not yet—but he was bold and increasingly defiant of anything that resembled control.

It became evident in how they dressed. Paul preferred neat, pressed clothes. Peter started choosing brighter colors, mismatched patterns, and styles that made him feel "different."

It was also visible in how they spent their time. Paul loved books and would spend hours lost in pages, asking deep questions about faith and purpose. Peter, however, preferred hands-on tasks—building, dismantling, exploring. He was the one who would climb the tree when everyone else stayed grounded.

Grace and Samuel watched the boys closely, amazed at how two children born minutes apart could be so different.

"They're like day and night," Samuel said one evening.

"They were never meant to be the same," Grace replied. "God gave us a leader and a firebrand."

School became the proving ground for their divergence. Paul was praised for discipline and cooperation. Peter received notes for "talking too much" or "being easily distracted."

And yet, both were brilliant in their own ways.

Paul earned recognition in the classroom.
Peter earned attention on the playground.
It wasn't that Peter was bad. It was that his spirit burned brighter—and wilder—than the spaces he was placed in. While Paul found peace in structure,

Peter began to push against every boundary.
Their sibling bond, though still intact, began to stretch. Small disagreements became frequent. Paul

would say, "Let's think this through." Peter would reply, "Let's just do it and see what happens."

But beneath the friction was still a sense of shared identity. They were brothers. Twins. Tied by blood, history, and moments too precious to erase.
Even if their paths were beginning to separate, their story was still one.
For now.

Peter's Growing Curiosity and Rebelliousness

Peter had always been curious, but as he moved into his pre-teen years, that curiosity took on a new edge. It was no longer about asking questions out of wonder—it was about challenging the answers he received. He began to push boundaries more deliberately, exploring the world beyond the tight circle of his parents' teachings and expectations.
"Why can't I watch what my friends watch?" he asked one evening, frowning as Grace turned off the TV during a scene she deemed inappropriate. "It's not that bad. Everyone at school talks about it."
"Because we are not everyone," Grace replied gently. "You are a child of God, Peter. What you feed your mind with matters."

"But what if I want to see for myself? What if I don't agree with everything the Bible says?"

Samuel, overhearing the exchange, set his book aside. "Peter, be careful. Questions are good, but pride in your own understanding can be dangerous." Peter shrugged, eyes narrowing. "I'm just saying—I want to make up my own mind."

And so began a season marked by testing limits. Peter started spending more time with boys who challenged authority just like he did.
He became fascinated with things that were off-limits—music with explicit lyrics, YouTube channels that mocked religion, online forums where opinions clashed with everything he'd been taught.

Grace noticed the change in his demeanor. He was still polite on the surface, but his tone often carried sarcasm. He responded to correction with eye rolls or silence. His once lively prayers became muttered and rare. He now mumbled grace at the dinner table instead of saying it with conviction.

At school, his teachers noted his growing defiance. "Peter is bright, but he's argumentative," one teacher said during a conference. "He questions everything—not out of curiosity, but to challenge authority. It's becoming disruptive."
Grace's heart sank, but Samuel bristled. "He must learn that freedom is not license. There are boundaries in life."

Peter, however, was fascinated by freedom. The idea that he could form his own beliefs, chart his own path, and reject anything that felt constricting thrilled him.

One day, he came home from school and tossed his Bible onto his desk carelessly.
"Why do we always have to read this?" he asked. "It's full of old stories. Some of them don't even make sense."
Paul, who was sitting quietly across the room, looked up. "Because it's God's Word."
Peter scoffed. "Or just a bunch of made-up rules. Who says God even wrote it?"
The words pierced Grace like a dagger. She called him into the living room, sat him down, and looked into his eyes.

"Peter, do you believe in God?" she asked softly.
Peter looked away. "I don't know anymore."
Samuel's hands clenched into fists. "Then you are forgetting who you are."
"No," Peter said quietly. "I'm trying to figure it out."
That night, Grace cried in her room while Samuel paced the floor in silence. They were witnessing the beginning of a departure they had long feared.

Peter's questions weren't all spiritual. He began probing into social issues, politics, and history—trying to understand the world outside the narrow scope he felt he had been raised within.

He argued with Samuel over the dinner table, questioned the sermons they heard at church, and began pulling away from family devotion time.
"Why should we follow something just because it's tradition?" he asked one evening when asked to lead the closing prayer.
"Because truth doesn't change," Samuel replied firmly.
"But people change," Peter said. "The world changes. Maybe we need to change too."

Grace watched him with mixed emotions. On one hand, she admired his intelligence and confidence. On the other, she feared where his restlessness might lead.

Paul remained steady in contrast. The more Peter pulled away, the more Paul pressed in—into his faith, into his studies, and into his quiet obedience. But even Paul began to feel the distance growing.
"You're not the same anymore," Paul said one afternoon. "You don't care about the things we used to care about."

"I still care," Peter replied. "I just don't want to be told how to think."

"But what if the truth isn't something you decide?" Peter looked at his brother, half amused, half tired. "Then maybe I need to find that out for myself."

Paul's Steady Faith and Developing Leadership Qualities

As Peter's voice grew louder and more resistant, Paul's became deeper, steadier, and more resolute—not in volume, but in conviction.

His quiet demeanor, once mistaken for timidity, began to reveal a strength of spirit that amazed even his parents. While Peter challenged everything, Paul chose to build—on truth, on discipline, and on the solid foundation of faith.

Grace noticed the transformation early. Paul began waking up before the rest of the family to spend time in prayer. He read his Bible not because he was told to, but because he desired to. Scriptures that others skimmed, he studied. Verses that were recited out of habit, he meditated upon.

"Why do you do all this on your own?" Grace asked him one morning, as she found him in the corner of the living room with his Bible open and a journal on his lap.

Paul looked up with his gentle eyes. "Because I want to know God for myself."

Samuel, though often consumed with work and Peter's defiance, began to take notice too. He watched Paul lead evening devotions with his mother, answer Bible trivia questions with precision, and ask insightful questions that revealed a mind deeply engaged.

"God is shaping this one," Samuel whispered to Grace one night. "He carries something sacred."
Paul's strength wasn't just in his knowledge—it was in his character. When classmates mocked other students, Paul stood apart. When temptations came in the form of peer pressure or subtle compromises, he walked away.

"Why don't you ever join in?" a boy asked during lunch. "You think you're better than us?"
"No," Paul replied calmly. "I just know who I want to be."

At church, his leadership began to bloom. He was asked to assist in teaching younger children, lead youth Bible studies, and help with organizing services. Though soft-spoken, his words carried weight. When he spoke, others listened.

"He doesn't lead with noise," the youth pastor once told Samuel and Grace. "He leads with presence. He lives what he believes. That's rare."

Paul's love for the Word translated into action. He started a small prayer group at school—just three students who met once a week during break time to pray quietly in a corner of the library. When others found out, some laughed. But Paul didn't stop.
"Even if I'm the only one," he told Grace, "I'll keep praying."
His leadership extended to home, though never forcefully. When Peter would lash out or argue, Paul responded with calm words or silence. Not because he had no response—but because he understood the power of restraint.
"I don't need to win arguments," Paul said. "I just want to live in peace."

Samuel, at times, struggled with how to relate to him. He was proud—but also uncertain how to father a son who seemed so mature.

"Don't let your gentleness be weakness," he cautioned one evening. "The world respects strength."
"I know, Papa," Paul said. "But strength isn't always loud. Jesus was strong—and He was gentle too."

Those words struck Samuel more deeply than he let on. He knew then that Paul wasn't just quoting scripture. He was living it.

Grace, meanwhile, continued to nurture Paul's gifts. She encouraged him to take speaking opportunities in church, to write devotionals, and to mentor younger children. His humility made him approachable, and his faith made him trustworthy.

But even Paul wasn't immune to the challenges of growing up. He sometimes felt isolated—different even among his peers at church. While others laughed loudly and fit in effortlessly, he often stood alone.
"Am I too serious?" he asked Grace one evening.
"No," she replied. "You are exactly who God made you to be. And that's more than enough."
His leadership wasn't about popularity; it was about purpose. And though he didn't always feel it, Paul was being prepared for more than he could imagine.

Family Outings, Interactions, and Misunderstandings

Family outings had always been a deliberate tradition for the Okafors—an intentional attempt by Samuel and Grace to preserve a sense of unity and joy amidst the demands of work, school, and faith. Whether it was a walk to the nearby Assiniboine Park, a trip to the zoo, or an occasional dinner at a modest Nigerian restaurant, these moments were meant to be a reset, a celebration of family.

But as the boys grew older, even these outings became strained. What was once a shared delight began to expose deeper rifts—between personalities, priorities, and perceptions.

One sunny Saturday afternoon, Grace had packed a picnic lunch and convinced the entire family to spend the day at the park. It was the kind of simple event she hoped would reignite closeness.
Peter grumbled as he pulled on his jacket. "Do we have to go? I had plans with friends."
"Family comes first," Samuel said sternly. "Your friends will still be there tomorrow."
Paul, as usual, made no fuss. He helped carry the food baskets to the car and even reminded Grace not to forget the blanket.

He genuinely looked forward to these moments. For him, they were a break from the noise of life, a chance to simply be.

At the park, the boys' differences played out in small but telling ways. Peter wandered off to explore on his own, eventually joining a group of neighborhood kids in a game of soccer. Paul sat with Grace, helping her unpack the food and asking her questions about Bible stories she hadn't yet shared. Samuel watched from a distance, his eyes following Peter. "He's drifting," he murmured to Grace. "Even here, he separates himself."

"He's searching," Grace said gently. "And he still came, didn't he?"

Later, as they gathered around to eat, tensions simmered under the surface. Paul thanked God for the meal in a soft but clear voice, while Peter rolled his eyes and mumbled a sarcastic "amen."

"Can you just be serious for one moment?" Samuel asked, the edge in his voice betraying his frustration. Peter shrugged. "I was serious. Just not in your way."

Grace quickly redirected the conversation to lighter topics, but the silence between father and son lingered.

Another outing to the mall revealed similar tension. While Grace and Paul were drawn to a Christian bookstore, Peter wandered into an electronics shop. When Samuel found him there watching a violent video game demonstration, his temper flared.

"What are you filling your mind with?" Samuel demanded.

"It's just a game," Peter snapped back. "You act like everything is evil."

"That's not the point," Samuel said, lowering his voice. "You should be wise with your choices."

Peter walked away without responding, leaving Samuel stewing in the tension.

Back at home, the rift between the brothers also showed itself in subtle ways. Paul would try to engage Peter in a conversation about a recent sermon or a memory verse, only for Peter to brush him off.

"Why do you always talk about church stuff?" Peter said one evening, slouched on the couch with headphones in. "Don't you ever think about anything else?"

"I do," Paul replied calmly. "But that's what matters most to me."

Peter scoffed. "You're just trying to impress Mom and Dad."

"No," Paul said. "I'm trying to live what I believe."

The misunderstanding between them ran deep. Peter viewed Paul's faith as performance. Paul viewed Peter's rebellion as a cry for attention. Both were partly right and partly wrong, but neither knew how to bridge the widening gap.

Even during family game nights—once a source of laughter and light-hearted competition—tensions could erupt. If Peter lost, he'd accuse Paul of cheating. If Paul won, Peter would accuse him of being smug. What had once bonded them now revealed how much they had changed.

Samuel and Grace tried to manage the tension. Samuel focused on discipline—talks, rules, and expectations. Grace focused on heart—prayers, conversations, and moments of connection. But more often than not, the misunderstandings outpaced their efforts.

"Maybe we've lost him," Samuel said one evening after Peter stormed off from a Bible trivia game.

"No," Grace replied, her eyes fixed on the closed door. "We haven't lost him. He's still watching us. Still listening. Even if he pretends not to."

Paul overheard and quietly slipped away, retreating to his journal. In it, he wrote a simple line:
"Sometimes love speaks loudest when it stays silent."

Family outings continued, but the innocence was gone. In its place stood the fragile hope that, in time, these fractured moments would lead to understanding, healing, and maybe—just maybe—a return to unity.

Conflicts Over Values and Expectations

As Peter and Paul moved further into adolescence, their once-close bond continued to unravel. The small tensions of childhood disagreements evolved into more serious confrontations, often centered around values, priorities, and expectations laid down by their parents.

It wasn't just that they liked different things. It was that they began to believe different things.
Peter questioned everything. Paul affirmed the old paths. And those opposing views, born under the same roof, began to collide with greater force.
One evening, during family devotion, Grace asked each son to share something they had learned recently from Scripture. Paul spoke first, referencing a parable from the book of Luke. He spoke with quiet clarity, drawing connections to everyday life and expressing how he wanted to model compassion and integrity.

When it was Peter's turn, he shrugged. "I didn't read anything."

Samuel's brow tightened. "Why not?"

"Because I don't see the point," Peter said bluntly. "It's the same stuff every time—be good, follow rules, pray. But real life isn't like that. People cheat, lie, steal, and they're still ahead."

Paul flinched at the cynicism in his brother's voice. "That's not true," he replied. "Doing what's right matters. God honors obedience."

"Easy for you to say," Peter snapped. "You've never had to stand out. You blend in with your Bible and your perfect grades. You don't get it."

"I'm not trying to be perfect," Paul said softly. "I'm just trying to please God."

"Well, I'm tired of trying to please everyone," Peter shot back, rising from the couch. "I'm going to live for myself."

He stormed out of the room, leaving behind a silence thick with tension. Grace closed her eyes and whispered a prayer beneath her breath.

The rift between the boys widened in school. Peter started associating with students who lived on the edge—ones who boasted about skipping classes, smoking behind the gym, and defying teachers.

Paul stuck with a quieter group, some from church, others who shared his love for reading and debate.
"Your brother is so fake," one of Peter's new friends commented one afternoon. "Acts like he's a saint or something."

Peter didn't defend Paul. He remained silent.
Later that week, Paul confronted him. "Why didn't you say anything when they mocked me?"
Peter avoided eye contact. "Because you are always trying to be better than everyone. It's annoying."
"I'm not trying to be better," Paul said. "I'm just trying to be right."
"Exactly," Peter snapped. "And that's the problem. You think you're always right."

Paul turned away, his heart heavy. He had never wanted a competition—only companionship. But it seemed that everything he did now irritated Peter.
Grace and Samuel tried to mediate, but their sons were becoming young men, and their differences no longer bowed easily to parental correction. At family dinners, Peter barely spoke unless provoked. When he did, his comments were often sarcastic or inflammatory.

"You know what Paul's real problem is?" Peter said one night, poking at his food. "He's scared to live.

He hides behind God because he's too afraid to make his own choices."

Paul set down his fork, visibly wounded. "No," he said. "I trust God because I've seen Him work. That's not fear. That's faith."
"Keep telling yourself that," Peter muttered.

Samuel slammed his hand on the table. "Enough. We are a family. We do not tear each other down."
But the words couldn't erase the growing chasm between the brothers. Their differences were now more than personality—they were foundational.
Paul believed life had purpose and order. Peter believed life was messy and to be taken on his own terms.

And though they still shared a room, their silence spoke louder than any shouting match.
At night, Grace would pray between their beds, one hand on each twin. Her whispered petitions filled the dark.
"Lord, make them one again. Let truth win Peter's heart. Let love guard Paul's."

But even as her tears fell onto their sleeping forms, she sensed that the battle between light and darkness, between obedience and rebellion, had only just begun.

Samuel and Grace's Efforts to Nurture Both Sons Despite Their Differences

Parenting twins had never been easy, but for Samuel and Grace, raising Peter and Paul had evolved into a full-time mission field—one filled with hope, heartbreak, prayer, and persistence. As their sons grew more distinct in values, interests, and behavior, the couple found themselves torn between discipline and understanding, correction and compassion.

They had raised them with the same prayers, under the same roof, with the same principles. Yet the outcome was no longer the same. One son leaned into faith, the other into independence. And Samuel and Grace had to adjust, daily, to nurture them both without alienating either.

Samuel, a man of strong convictions, initially found Peter's rebellion deeply disappointing. He viewed it as a personal failure—a stain on his efforts as a father and spiritual leader.
"I've taught him the Word," Samuel would lament. "I've prayed with him, spoken with him, disciplined him. What else is there to do?"

Grace, ever the bridge between the fire of Samuel's discipline and the chill of Peter's defiance, would respond gently. "We do what we've always done—we love him. We pray. And we do not give up."

While Samuel struggled with Peter's resistance, he also feared becoming too harsh. He had seen the way Peter shut down when scolded. So, he began trying something new—conversations instead of lectures.

He started sitting with Peter, not just to correct, but to listen. They'd talk while fixing things in the garage, watching sports, or during long drives.

"You're smart," Samuel told him one evening. "And I know you want to make your own choices. But son, freedom without direction is destruction."

Peter didn't always reply, but he listened more when Samuel was calm. The effort was slow, inconsistent, but Samuel clung to the possibility that Peter's heart might still be soft beneath the bravado.

With Paul, Samuel's challenge was different. He feared smothering the boy with expectations. Paul was responsible and obedient, but Samuel didn't want him to become burdened by perfectionism or performance.

"You don't always have to have the answers," he told Paul one night. "God's not measuring you by your output. He loves you because you're His."

Paul nodded, the words sinking deep. He had carried the weight of being the "good son" for so long, and his father's reassurance gave him a breath of grace.

Grace, meanwhile, was the family's emotional anchor. She continued to hold family devotions, prepare meals with Scripture verses tucked under plates, and pray over her sons while they slept. Her love was persistent, unshaken by their drift.

She found creative ways to connect with Peter—asking his opinion on things he liked, inviting his friends over for dinner, and never using guilt as a weapon.

"Peter, I may not always agree with you," she once said. "But I will always fight for you in prayer."

Her words weren't dramatic; they were consistent. Over time, Peter began to open up to her in small ways—about his struggles at school, his doubts about faith, and his fears of not being understood.

With Paul, Grace continued to pour encouragement into his budding leadership. She challenged him to lead by love, not pride. When Paul grew frustrated with Peter's behavior, she reminded him: "Even Jesus loved those who rejected Him. Your strength is in your ability to still love Peter, even when he won't listen."

There were still tough days. Days when Peter slammed doors, skipped devotions, or answered questions with silence. Days when Paul felt invisible or burdened with holding the moral line. Days when Samuel doubted if any of it was making a difference. But Grace held onto one truth: God had not failed them.

Every night, she and Samuel knelt beside their bed, hands clasped.

"Lord, You gave us these boys. Help us to raise them in wisdom and love. Soften Peter's heart. Strengthen Paul's walk. And help us not to give up when we are weary."

They knew that parenting wasn't about controlling outcomes—it was about remaining faithful in the process. And even as their sons' paths diverged, Samuel and Grace were determined to walk with both, believing that love, patience, and prayer would one day bring them back together.

Introduction of Friendships That Influence Peter and Paul in Opposing Ways

As Peter and Paul continued to grow, the people they chose to surround themselves with began to shape them in ways Samuel and Grace could not always control. Where parental influence once held the most sway, now the voices of friends grew louder—affirming, challenging, and even steering the boys toward choices that would further define their paths.

Peter was drawn to energy—people who were bold, daring, and unapologetically free. One of those influences was Jamal, a boy from their school who lived a few blocks away. Jamal was charismatic and street-smart, with a swagger that captivated Peter almost immediately.

"He's cool," Peter told Paul one afternoon. "He knows what he wants and doesn't let anyone boss him around."

"But he skips class," Paul pointed out. "And he talks back to teachers."

"Exactly," Peter replied with a grin. "He doesn't take nonsense from anyone."

Jamal introduced Peter to a world of edgy humor, rebellious talk, and a growing disdain for structure.

They shared playlists full of music Grace would never approve of and hung out in corners of the neighborhood where authority was mocked and rules were considered optional.

"Your parents don't own you," Jamal once said. "They had their chance. Now it's your life."

Peter didn't fully believe those words at first, but they echoed in his mind during moments of frustration. Slowly, Jamal's philosophies began to feel like a validation of Peter's doubts.

Meanwhile, Paul's circle formed in a completely different space. At church, he grew close to Jonathan, the pastor's son—a gentle, thoughtful boy who shared Paul's love for scripture, music, and purposeful living. Jonathan wasn't loud or particularly popular, but he was consistent, and that consistency made Paul feel safe.

"Don't worry about being different," Jonathan once told him after a youth Bible study. "We're not called to blend in. We're called to shine."

Paul smiled, the words strengthening his quiet resolve.

The two began working together on youth projects, volunteering during services, and organizing weekend outreach events. They shared books, fasted together, and challenged each other to grow spiritually.

Grace observed the difference in her sons' friendships with an attentive heart. She met Jonathan and immediately approved. She could see the purity of heart and intentionality he brought into Paul's life.
"Stick with boys like him," she told Paul one evening. "Iron sharpens iron. And he will sharpen you."

But she had deep concerns about Jamal. Peter grew more secretive, more irritable, and more dismissive of authority. His grades began to slip. He often came home late and gave vague excuses about where he'd been.
"I don't like the path he's on," Samuel confessed after Peter was caught lying about his whereabouts. "That boy, Jamal—he's trouble."
"I've tried to warn him," Grace said. "But Peter says Jamal listens to him when no one else does."
"That's because Jamal tells him what he wants to hear."

The contrast between the brothers grew sharper. Paul started mentoring younger boys at church. He and Jonathan hosted a small prayer group every Thursday evening in the church basement.

Peter, on the other hand, began spending weekends at a local arcade with Jamal and others—places where profanity flew freely and values were mocked. When Paul invited Peter to one of their youth events, Peter laughed. "You want me to come sing songs and talk about feelings? No thanks. I've got real things to do."

Jonathan, though hurt, remained gracious. "We'll be here when you're ready."
But Peter didn't want to be ready. He wanted to run. To explore. To rebel. And Jamal offered him a road with fewer rules and more adventure.
Paul, however, continued to walk a quieter, narrower path, strengthened by the quiet accountability of a faithful friend.

Moments of Connection and Alienation Between the Brothers

Though Peter and Paul now lived more like roommates than brothers, there were still flickers of their old bond—fleeting moments where something deeper broke through the walls of pride, frustration, and silence. Moments that reminded both of them—and their parents—that love had not been extinguished, only buried.

It was a cold winter afternoon when the first of those rare moments emerged.
The furnace had gone out, and the entire house shivered in silence while Samuel waited for the repairman. The boys were home from school, layered in hoodies and blankets.
Paul, huddled on the living room floor with a flashlight, was reading a devotional book. Peter sat nearby, scrolling through his phone with frozen fingers.
"Your hands are shaking," Paul said quietly, breaking the silence.
Peter shrugged. "It's freezing."

Without a word, Paul stood up, went to his room, and returned with an extra pair of gloves. He tossed them gently onto Peter's lap.
Peter looked up, surprised. "Thanks," he mumbled.

Paul nodded and sat back down. No sermon, no lecture. Just warmth.

For a moment, they sat in peace—brothers, if only in silence.

But such moments were rare.

More often than not, the distance between them seemed to grow with each passing day. At church, Paul was praised for his leadership in the youth group, often asked to lead prayers or present lessons.

Peter, if he attended at all, sat in the back with crossed arms and a guarded scowl.

"You act like you've got it all figured out," Peter said one evening after dinner. "Like God chose you and forgot about the rest of us."

Paul was stunned. "That's not true. I'm just doing what I believe is right."

"Yeah, and you never let anyone forget it."

"That's not fair," Paul said, his voice quiet but hurt. "I don't flaunt it. I just live it."

"Well, it feels like you're judging me every time you breathe," Peter snapped, storming off.

Grace overheard and found Paul sitting alone at the dining table.

"He's angry," she said, placing a hand on his shoulder.

Paul sighed. "And I don't know how to fix it."

"You're not supposed to fix him," she replied. "You're supposed to love him."

Another glimmer of connection came unexpectedly one rainy afternoon. Peter had twisted his ankle during a pickup game and limped home drenched and frustrated. Paul, arriving moments later from the church library, found him sitting on the porch, wincing in pain.

Without saying a word, Paul helped him inside, grabbed an ice pack, and wrapped the injury in a towel.

"Don't tell Dad," Peter muttered. "He'll say it's what I get for skipping choir practice."
Paul chuckled softly. "Mum's the word."
Peter looked at him and, for a second, seemed ready to speak. But the words stayed lodged in his throat.
"Thanks," he said.
Paul simply nodded.

Yet the walls between them remained. Peter refused to attend Paul's school debates, and Paul stopped inviting him after a while. Peter missed Paul's birthday dinner, saying he had "plans." Paul didn't mention it again, but he spent that night in prayer.
"I miss my brother," he wrote in his journal. "Not the one he is now, but the one we used to be."

Samuel and Grace saw the dance of connection and alienation play out like clockwork. Small acts of kindness would show up unannounced, like Peter fixing Paul's broken headphone wire or Paul saving a slice of meat pie for Peter after youth meetings. But they never talked about these gestures.

"Pride is a cruel wall," Samuel said one night.
"Love is a stronger hammer," Grace replied.

There was hope in the stillness. Hope that beneath the disagreements and the pain, the bond of brotherhood hadn't been lost—only tested.
And in the quiet spaces between the storms, a seed of reconciliation still waited to bloom.

Chapter Four:

The Call of Rebellion

The Choices We Make: Seeds of Destiny

Peter's Entrance into Adolescence: Increased Defiance and Questioning of Authority

Adolescence hit Peter like a storm. The once-playful child who had a sparkle in his eye now wore a cloud of questions, attitude, and defiance like a second skin. His voice deepened, his expressions sharpened, and his curiosity transformed into open rebellion.
Samuel and Grace had anticipated challenges, but nothing prepared them for the emotional rollercoaster Peter was becoming.

Rules that once went unquestioned were now met with resistance. Morning devotion became a battleground. Chores were done reluctantly, if at all. Conversations turned into debates, and debates turned into arguments.

"I don't see why we have to keep doing this family devotion," Peter declared one morning, slumped in his chair, arms folded. "It's just the same verses over and over again."
"It's not about repetition," Samuel replied, trying to keep his tone even. "It's about discipline. It's about building a habit of hearing God's voice."
"What if I'm not even sure I believe all this anymore?"

The room fell silent. Paul looked down at his Bible, hurt flashing across his face.

Grace spoke gently, "Peter, you don't have to understand everything now. But trust what you've been taught."

"But what if what I've been taught isn't enough?" he shot back. "What if I want to find my own truth?"

That phrase—*my own truth*—became Peter's new anthem. It was the shield he raised any time someone tried to correct, guide, or discipline him. He questioned authority at home, at school, and at church.

Teachers reported growing disrespect in class. He began interrupting lessons, talking back, and challenging ideas with a confidence that bordered on arrogance.

"He's bright," one teacher said during a school meeting. "But he's becoming disruptive. It's like he's more interested in proving a point than learning anything."

Samuel was torn. He recognized in Peter a sharp mind and strong will—traits he himself had once been praised for. But without submission to godly guidance, those strengths were becoming dangerous weaknesses.

At church, Peter grew distant. He still attended—largely to avoid confrontation—but he no longer engaged. He stopped singing, ignored the messages, and often snuck out before service ended.

When the youth pastor tried to encourage him, Peter replied, "I don't need another adult telling me how to live. I already get that at home."

Grace's heart ached. She saw her son pulling away, not just from them but from the foundation they had laid with prayer, love, and intention.

"He's searching," she told Samuel one night, tears brimming in her eyes. "But I'm afraid of what he's finding."

Peter's appearance began to change too. He experimented with new styles—baggy clothes, hooded sweatshirts, and accessories that clashed with his once-simplistic demeanor. His language became edgier, his sense of humor darker.

But perhaps the most alarming change was Peter's growing resistance to correction. What used to be a simple rebuke now sparked hours of tension.

One evening, after Samuel asked him to turn off a violent video game, Peter exploded.

"You don't control my life!" he shouted. "I'm not a child anymore. You can't keep forcing your beliefs down my throat."

Samuel stood silent for a moment, then replied, "No, I can't force you. But I can refuse to let you destroy yourself under my roof."
Peter grabbed his phone and stormed into his room, slamming the door so hard it echoed through the house.

Paul later found him sitting on the edge of his bed, headphones on, expression blank.
"Are you okay?" Paul asked.
Peter pulled off one headphone and gave a tired look. "Don't start."
"I'm not here to fight," Paul said. "I just miss the old Peter."
"There's no 'old' or 'new' me," Peter muttered. "This is who I am now."

But even as he said it, there was a flicker of uncertainty in his eyes.
Peter's rebellion wasn't just about anger—it was about identity. He was trying to understand who he was outside of his family's shadow. But in pushing away the light of their love and faith, he was beginning to drift into dangerous darkness.

Samuel and Grace knew they were witnessing the first wave of a deeper battle.

And though Peter no longer looked to them for direction, they refused to stop watching, praying, and believing.
Because even prodigals have a home waiting.

Paul's Deepening Commitment to His Faith and Academic Excellence

As Peter drifted further from the family's spiritual compass, Paul anchored himself more deeply into the very truths his brother questioned. While Peter's rebellion brought chaos, Paul's commitment brought structure, reverence, and resilience.

Faith was no longer just a family routine for Paul—it had become his own language of life. He prayed more fervently, read scripture not for obligation but for direction, and often journaled his reflections in a small notebook Grace had given him on his twelfth birthday.

"Lord," he wrote one evening, "help me to remain steadfast. Even when it's lonely. Even when my brother mocks me. Help me to love him and never lose sight of Your purpose for me."

At school, Paul's diligence began to shine. He wasn't flashy about his achievements, but his teachers took notice.

He excelled in mathematics and literature, often praised for his sharp thinking and quiet leadership. When group work was assigned, classmates gravitated toward him not just because of his intellect, but because he was dependable.
"He's a quiet leader," one teacher noted. "The kind who influences without demanding attention."

He balanced school and faith with remarkable discipline. In addition to attending youth Bible study, he began tutoring younger students at church and mentoring one or two boys who looked up to him.
"He reminds me of Timothy," Grace once said to Samuel. "Faithful from his youth."

But Paul's strength was tested often—especially when he saw his parents heartbroken over Peter's choices. He heard their whispered prayers behind closed doors, saw the worry etched in Samuel's face and the tears in Grace's eyes.

"Should I do more?" he once asked Grace quietly. "Should I try harder to talk to Peter?"
"You're already doing more than you know," she replied. "Every time you love him without judgment, you plant a seed."

Paul didn't respond, but he nodded. His shoulders bore more than just academic expectations—he carried spiritual responsibility too. But rather than crumble, he leaned into it.

Still, he remained a teenager. There were moments of doubt, when he wished his path was easier, when he felt the weight of being the example. But in those moments, he turned to prayer and the Word. He memorized scriptures like anchors:

"Be strong and of a good courage; be not afraid, neither be thou dismayed: for the LORD thy God is with thee whithersoever thou goest." (Joshua 1:9)

Paul wasn't perfect—but he was grounded. And even as Peter spiraled into rebellion, Paul rose in wisdom, like a candle that refused to be extinguished.
He had chosen his path. And while it was narrow, it was lit with purpose.

Peter's Attraction to Peers Who Encourage His Rebelliousness

It wasn't long before Peter found himself gravitating toward a circle of friends who mirrored his growing defiance. These were not necessarily bad kids in the obvious sense—they didn't wear gang colors or commit crimes in the open—but they shared a common trait that Peter found irresistible: they didn't care about rules.

Jamal, DeShawn, and Liam were his closest companions. Each came from different backgrounds, but they bonded over their mutual disdain for adult expectations and authority. They skipped classes, pushed boundaries with teachers, and laughed at anything that reeked of discipline or tradition.

"They act like they know what's best for us," Jamal would often say, nodding toward their teachers or parents. "But they don't. We have to figure it out for ourselves."

To Peter, these words were not just appealing—they were liberating. In this group, he didn't have to pretend. He could roll his eyes at sermons, ignore his parents' curfews, and dismiss Paul's quiet devotion without feeling judged.

With these peers, rebellion became a shared identity. They mocked those who followed the rules, labeled obedience as weakness, and treated questions of morality with sarcasm.

"You still go to church?" Liam once asked Peter with a smirk. "Man, that's old-school. My parents don't even bother anymore."

Peter laughed it off, even though a part of him still respected his family's faith. But respect was no longer his driving force—acceptance was. He desperately wanted to belong, to be seen as bold and independent. And if that meant distancing himself from everything he had been taught, so be it.

It started with skipping family devotions. Then it turned into making up excuses to avoid youth services. Soon, Peter stopped praying altogether.

Grace noticed the shift in his spirit, the coldness that seemed to settle over his eyes.

"Peter," she said gently one evening, "your friends—do they help you grow?"

"They help me be real," he replied flatly. "Not everyone wants to live in a bubble."

Samuel, more direct in his concern, sat him down another night. "I've seen where this road leads. These boys you follow—are they leading you to life, or to ruin?"

Peter folded his arms. "They let me breathe. That's more than I can say about this house."

It was the kind of response that broke Samuel's heart but deepened his resolve to keep praying.

The more time Peter spent with his new crew, the more he adopted their mindset. He started using language that had never before passed his lips. His wardrobe changed. His posture shifted. And though he was still under his parents' roof, it was clear that he had emotionally moved out.

The group gave him a sense of control he didn't feel at home. They listened when he talked, laughed at his jokes, and cheered him on when he challenged a teacher or ignored school rules.

"They get me," Peter told Paul one day, the tension between them simmering. "Unlike this place."

"They agree with your worst instincts," Paul replied. "That's not friendship—that's manipulation."

"You wouldn't understand," Peter snapped. "You've always done what you're told. You don't know what it's like to want to be free."

"But what's freedom if it leads you into bondage?" Paul asked quietly.

Peter had no answer. Or perhaps, he wasn't ready to admit it.

There were moments, fleeting and rare, when Peter felt the ache of something missing. Like when one of his friends got arrested for shoplifting, or when Jamal's father was taken into custody after a violent altercation. In those moments, Peter felt a cold fear rise in his chest—but he pushed it down, told himself he was different.

"I've got this under control," he whispered one night as he looked at himself in the mirror.

But deep inside, he wasn't sure.

Samuel's Frustration and Attempts to Guide Peter Back on Track

Samuel had always been a man of structure and resolve. A firm believer in the principles of hard work, faith, and family legacy, he had poured everything he had into building a stable life for his family in a land that had never quite felt like home. And now, watching his firstborn son spiral into rebellion, he felt like all that effort was unraveling before his eyes.

Each time Peter stormed out of a conversation, disobeyed a simple instruction, or came home later than allowed, Samuel's heart tightened. He wasn't just frustrated—he was afraid. Afraid of losing his son to a culture that made rebellion look like freedom. Afraid of watching history repeat itself through brokenness he had seen in others.

"He's slipping further away," Samuel told Grace one night. "And I don't know how to reach him."
"You reach him by being present," Grace answered softly. "By staying near, even when he pushes you away."

Samuel tried. He started carving out time in his schedule just to be around Peter—waiting up for him after outings, asking him to join in errands, even inviting him to help fix things around the house.
"Come help me in the garage," he'd say. "I need a strong hand."
Sometimes Peter came. Most times he didn't.

When they did spend time together, conversations were awkward. Peter would shrug or mumble answers, often distracted by his phone or earbuds. Still, Samuel persisted.

One day, as they changed the oil in the car, Samuel said, "You know, when I was your age, I had friends who promised the world but disappeared when things got hard."
Peter didn't respond.

"I made mistakes," Samuel continued. "Big ones. And I carried the scars for years. But God gave me a second chance. I just don't want you to need the same rescue I did."

Peter looked up briefly, then returned to tightening a bolt. "I'm not you, Dad."
"No," Samuel replied. "But I see myself in you. And I see the danger too."

Sometimes Samuel's frustration boiled over. Like the evening Peter came home smelling of cigarettes, shrugging off any explanation.
"This is not who we raised you to be!" Samuel shouted. "Do you want to destroy everything you've been given?"
Peter rolled his eyes. "You mean all the pressure? All the rules? Maybe I do!"

Samuel's voice cracked. "You're throwing away your future!"
Peter walked off, slamming his door.
That night, Samuel sat alone in the living room, his head in his hands.
"I don't want to be his enemy," he whispered to Grace. "But it feels like everything I say pushes him further."

Grace knelt beside him. "Then stop trying to fix him with your words. Let your love speak louder."
He took her advice. He stopped preaching and started praying more. He began writing short notes and leaving them on Peter's nightstand.

"I believe in you. I still see the greatness in you."
"You are not alone, no matter what path you walk."
"Come home—not just to us, but to yourself."

He started listening more, speaking less. Not because he had given up, but because he realized that rebellion didn't always need rebuke—it often needed refuge.

One night, Samuel walked past Peter's room and saw the boy sitting quietly, one of the notes in his hand.
He didn't say anything.
But Samuel closed his eyes and thanked God. Maybe—just maybe—the bridge hadn't collapsed. Maybe there was still time to repair it, one plank of love and patience at a time.

Grace's Quiet Prayers and Maternal Worry

Grace had always been the still voice in their home—the gentle anchor that steadied the ship when storms began to rise. Her strength was not loud, but it was deep. Her eyes missed nothing, and her heart carried the weight of every shift in the atmosphere of their home, especially when it came to Peter.

She had birthed him in faith, raised him with songs of worship, and taught him to pray before he could speak in full sentences. She had watched him learn to walk, watched him fall, watched him get up. But now, as he walked farther away from everything she had poured into him, she found herself kneeling more often than standing.

Grace was not quick to argue. Unlike Samuel, who met Peter's rebellion with direct confrontation, Grace turned to a different kind of warfare—intercession.

In the quiet hours of the night, when the house was still and the air was heavy, Grace knelt beside Peter's door and prayed.

"Lord, wherever he is tonight, keep him. Don't let darkness swallow his light. Speak to him even when he won't listen to us."

She slipped prayer notes into his Bible, into his jacket pockets, into his notebooks. Some he tossed aside. Others, he found much later—often when he needed them most.

One note simply read, *"You are still loved. Nothing you do can erase that."*

She fasted often—not just for Peter's return to faith, but for the wisdom to love him well in the meantime.

At church, she would linger at the altar long after the service had ended, tears sliding silently down her cheeks.

"Don't give up," one elder told her once. "Even the prodigal son came home."

"But what if he never leaves the far country?" she whispered.

"Then keep the light on. Keep the table set. Keep the robe ready."

Still, her worry grew.

Peter's laughter had changed. It wasn't full anymore—it was sharp, sarcastic. His smile was less frequent. And when he did speak to her, it was often in defense or dismissal.

"You don't understand me," he told her once.

"I don't need to understand everything," she replied gently. "I only need to love you."

Paul noticed too. He saw the weight his mother carried. Some evenings, he would sit beside her as she wept in prayer.

"God hears you," he told her.

"I know," she said with a tired smile. "But it still hurts."

Grace continued to serve in the church. She continued to cook Peter's favorite meals even when he didn't say thank you.

She continued to buy him new clothes even when he claimed he didn't need her. Not because he deserved it—but because that's what love does. It stays.

Her prayers were filled with scripture:

"And I will contend with him that contendeth with thee, and I will save thy children." (Isaiah 49:25)

She quoted it over Peter's pillow. She whispered it over his laundry. She declared it during morning devotions, even when he refused to join in.

"Peter will not be lost," she told Samuel one night. "I will not let go. God gave him to us, and I will fight until he returns."

And though her hands trembled, her faith did not. She knew the path of rebellion well. It was a winding one, full of ditches and deception. But she also knew the power of grace. She had seen it transform before—and she would believe until the end that it could transform her son.

The Role of the Church Community in Shaping Paul's Values

While Peter's steps carried him further into defiance, Paul found deeper footing in the church—the place that had always felt like home to him. The walls of the sanctuary, the cadence of Sunday hymns, the rhythm of Scripture and fellowship—these things didn't just ground him; they shaped him.

The church community played a powerful, almost parental role in Paul's development. The youth pastor, Brother Mark, quickly became one of Paul's most trusted mentors. He was not only a teacher but a man of character who modeled humility, accountability, and genuine love for God.
"Leadership isn't about being loud," Brother Mark told him once after a youth Bible study. "It's about living your faith so clearly that others follow you even when you're not speaking."

Those words settled into Paul's heart. They affirmed what he had always believed—that quiet strength was still strength.

Sister Naomi, a wise and warm woman in her sixties, also took an interest in Paul. She often invited him to join the intercessory prayer group.

At first, Paul hesitated—he didn't think he was "spiritual enough." But Naomi saw something in him.
"Intercession isn't for the perfect," she said. "It's for the willing."

Under her guidance, Paul learned the discipline of prayer, fasting, and sensitivity to the Holy Spirit. She taught him how to pray for others, how to listen for God's whisper, and how to remain humble even when praised.

The church also gave him opportunity. Paul was asked to share short devotions during youth gatherings. At first, his voice trembled, and his hands fidgeted. But over time, he grew more confident—because he knew what he believed, and he spoke from a place of conviction.

One Sunday morning, after delivering a message on the faith of David, an elderly man in the congregation pulled him aside.
"You remind me of Timothy," he said, tears in his eyes. "Don't let this world dim your fire."
That moment stayed with Paul.

The community also protected him. When rumors of Peter's behavior reached the church, many people began to whisper.

But the leaders quickly shut it down.
"This is not a place for gossip," Brother Mark said firmly during a leadership meeting. "This is a place for grace. Let's lift the Okafor family in prayer, not judgment."

Paul felt that shield around him. The people he served with never mocked him for his brother's choices. Instead, they rallied around him with encouragement.
"You're not responsible for Peter," Sister Naomi told him. "You just keep walking your path. And keep leaving a trail he can follow when he's ready."

The church wasn't perfect—no community is. But it was consistent. It was loving. It reinforced everything Samuel and Grace had tried to build at home.

It gave Paul a sense of belonging, a framework for his identity, and a vision for his future. In a world that was constantly shifting, the church remained his anchor.
And though Peter had tuned out the voices from the pulpit, Paul heard them clearly—and they shaped the man he was becoming.

Peter's Rejection of Religious Teachings

Peter had not always rejected religion. In his early years, he had bowed his head during prayers, memorized scriptures with Paul, and sang hymns with the children's choir. But as the tides of adolescence swept through his mind, the certainty of faith began to feel like a prison rather than a foundation.

To Peter, religion became synonymous with rules—an endless list of things not to do. And as his curiosity grew, so did his resentment.
"What's the point of all this?" he asked one evening after dinner, as the family gathered for evening devotion.
Samuel paused mid-reading. "The point, son, is to know God and live by His word."
Peter scoffed. "Or to keep people under control."
Grace looked up slowly, her voice calm. "Peter, the Word gives life. It gives direction."
Peter stood, eyes sharp. "It gives guilt. And fear. You keep telling me God loves me, but all I hear is what I'll be punished for if I step out of line."
The room fell silent.

From that moment on, Peter's posture toward religion hardened. He stopped attending church voluntarily. He tuned out sermons.

His Bible gathered dust on the shelf. He no longer bowed his head in prayer, even at family meals.

At school, he began to mock Christian beliefs openly.

"Faith is for people too afraid to face reality," he told a classmate who invited him to a youth event. "I'd rather deal with the truth—even if it's ugly."

The irony wasn't lost on Paul. Watching his brother dismantle everything they had grown up believing was painful.

"You used to believe," Paul said one night. "You used to pray."

"I used to believe in Santa Claus too," Peter replied flatly. "Some things just stop making sense."

Peter found new philosophies online—videos and forums where people questioned the Bible, discredited miracles, and labeled faith as a crutch for the weak. He soaked it all in.

One day, after school, he tossed his Bible into the trash can outside their apartment building. Grace found it hours later, stained and torn from rain.

She didn't say a word when Peter came home. She simply placed the Bible on the table and whispered, "It's still the Word of God, even when you're angry with it."

Peter didn't respond.
Samuel tried to confront him again, but Peter's guard was too high.

"You want me to believe in a God who watches people suffer and do nothing?" Peter shouted. "You say He has a plan, but what kind of plan includes pain and silence?"
Samuel clenched his jaw. "It's not our place to judge the Creator."
Peter rolled his eyes. "Maybe it's not your place to question Him. But it is mine."

Paul stood in the corner, his fists balled. He wanted to speak, to argue, but something in Peter's face stopped him. His brother wasn't rebelling for the sake of mischief anymore—he was breaking. Wrestling. Searching.

That night, Grace wept silently in her room.
"He's not lost," she whispered to Samuel. "He's just wounded. And wounds don't heal by force—they heal by grace."

Peter's rejection of religion wasn't just intellectual—it was emotional. He felt betrayed by the faith that had been used as both shield and sword.

In his mind, it had become a cage. And like a caged bird, he thrashed wildly, not realizing he was breaking his wings in the process.

Increasing Tension Between the Brothers and Their Parents

The once warm and cohesive atmosphere of the Okafor household had grown colder. Conversations were shorter, glances more guarded, and silence more frequent. The tension that had once simmered beneath the surface was now impossible to ignore.

Peter's rebelliousness had taken center stage, but it wasn't only Peter who struggled. The family dynamic had shifted. Every interaction felt like navigating a minefield, especially between the brothers and their parents.

Samuel and Peter were the most combustible. Samuel's values clashed directly with Peter's new worldview, and their exchanges often ended in raised voices and slammed doors.

"You think you know everything," Samuel said one evening after Peter refused to help with family chores.
"I just don't want to be controlled," Peter fired back.
"This is not control—it's structure!"

"To you, maybe. To me, it's oppression."

Grace would step in, trying to calm the storm, but her words were often drowned out in the heat of argument. Peter accused them of favoritism, convinced that Paul's obedience was praised while his struggles were condemned.

"I make one mistake and it's the end of the world," he said. "But Paul does the same thing and gets a Bible verse of encouragement."
"That's not true," Grace said, hurt flashing in her eyes. "We love both of you equally."
"Then stop expecting me to be him," Peter snapped.

Paul, meanwhile, was caught in the crossfire. His loyalty to his parents and his growing disapproval of Peter's choices put him in an impossible position. Conversations between him and Peter became strained, and Paul's attempts at peace often made things worse.
"You think I don't see it?" Peter said to Paul during one argument. "You're the golden boy. You can do no wrong. They worship the ground you walk on."
"That's not fair," Paul replied. "I just try to do what's right."
"Exactly. You try so hard to be perfect, and it makes me look worse."

"That's not my fault."
"But it feels like it."

Even meals, once a time of laughter and bonding, became tense. Peter would sit in silence, stabbing his food with his fork while Samuel prayed. Paul tried to hold conversations, but the atmosphere was too heavy.
"Can we just eat without the drama?" Peter asked one evening, tossing his napkin aside.
"You bring the drama," Samuel responded sharply.
Paul reached for Grace's hand under the table. She squeezed it but said nothing.

The home that had once been filled with singing, laughter, and storytelling now echoed with quiet heartbreak. Grace prayed more. Samuel watched Peter more closely. Paul journaled late into the night.
Each member of the family was doing what they could to hold things together, but the threads were fraying.

Peter's distance felt like betrayal. Paul's example felt like pressure. Samuel's authority felt like control. Grace's gentleness felt like silence.
And yet, love remained. Fragile, bruised, but present.

Chapter Five:

The Road Less Traveled

Peter's First Major Act of Rebellion: A Critical Turning Point

It began on an ordinary Thursday afternoon—one of those days that bore no warning of the storm to come. The sky was clear, school had just let out, and Peter should have been heading home. But instead of boarding the usual bus with Paul, he slipped out through the back gate, joining Jamal and a few others who had a plan.

"Let's go," Jamal said, his voice laced with challenge. "Today's the day."

They weren't headed anywhere productive. Their destination was a strip mall where they'd scoped out a small electronics shop known for its inattentive staff. Jamal had dared Peter to prove his independence—to step beyond the edge and show he wasn't just talk.

"You say you're your own man," Jamal had smirked. "Let's see it."

What started as peer pressure turned into an unshakable temptation. Peter's mind buzzed with rebellion and adrenaline. It wasn't just about the headphones Jamal suggested he swipe—it was about the statement.

He didn't need permission. He didn't need religion. He didn't need his father's approval.

So he did it.

With shaky hands and a pounding heart, Peter slipped the boxed earbuds into his hoodie and walked out, trying to act casual, though every step felt like a drumbeat announcing his guilt.
The store owner wasn't fooled.

Minutes later, two police officers approached them at the corner. Jamal bolted. Peter froze.
The walk to the station was silent. Peter refused to speak until Samuel arrived—his face a mixture of fury and heartbreak.
"You stole?" Samuel's voice trembled, not from anger, but disbelief. "Peter... why?"
Peter stared at the floor. "Because I could."

The officers let him go with a warning, noting it was his first offense. But the consequences reached far beyond legal reprimand. That night, their home shifted permanently.
Grace wept for hours. Paul sat on the stairs, unsure if he should comfort his mother or go confront his brother. Samuel paced the living room, his hands on his head, muttering scriptures to steady his mind.
When he finally sat Peter down, the words didn't come immediately.

"You are not just a boy who made a mistake," Samuel said finally. "You are a boy walking into destruction with his eyes wide open."

Peter's expression remained cold, but inside, something cracked. The sight of Grace crying, of Paul's disappointment, of his father's trembling hands—it all haunted him.
Still, pride kept him from apologizing. Instead, he doubled down, staying out later, refusing to eat with the family, and spending more time with Jamal and his crowd.
But something had shifted. This wasn't just rebellion anymore—it was identity. A crossroads.

That theft marked more than a moment of wrongdoing. It was the first undeniable fracture in his relationship with the values that had once defined his life. It was the turning point, not just for Peter—but for everyone who loved him.

Paul's Achievements in School and Church

While Peter's rebellion cast a shadow over the household, Paul's light continued to shine with quiet consistency. He didn't seek attention or praise, yet both found him. Amid the turbulence at home, Paul became a source of calm—steady in his faith, disciplined in his studies, and increasingly admired by those around him.

At school, his teachers spoke of him with respect.

"Paul is a model student," one said during a parent-teacher conference. "He listens attentively, asks thoughtful questions, and helps his classmates without being asked."

Paul had maintained straight A's across all his subjects for the third consecutive year. His essays in English class were often read aloud by his teacher as examples of clarity and insight. In science, he led a team that won second place in a regional project fair for a study on renewable energy.

His teachers weren't the only ones who took notice.

The school principal invited Paul to serve on the student leadership committee, and he was often called upon to represent his class in public speaking competitions and academic showcases.

He remained humble through it all.

"I'm just doing my part," he would say whenever someone praised him. "It's not about being the best—it's about being faithful."

At church, Paul's growth was just as evident. He became a respected youth in the congregation—mature beyond his years, but always approachable.

He taught Sunday school classes to younger children, organized youth Bible trivia nights, and regularly led prayer sessions.

"Paul has a pastor's heart," Sister Naomi once whispered to Grace. "There's oil on that boy's life." During a youth revival service, Paul was asked to share a message. His sermon, titled *"The Cost of Consistency"*, drew tears from many in the audience. He spoke not with charisma, but with conviction, drawing from his own journey of obedience amid personal trials.

"Being consistent doesn't mean you have no doubts," he said. "It means you choose faith, even when it's hard."

The church elders were so impressed that they began mentoring him for greater leadership roles. Some even suggested that Paul consider seminary in the future.

But Paul didn't get carried away with the applause. At home, he continued helping Grace in the kitchen, quietly encouraging his father, and praying—fervently—for Peter.

One afternoon, while cleaning the church sanctuary after service, Brother Mark approached him.
"You're doing more than most grown men do," he said. "But never forget: your first ministry is your family. Don't stop loving your brother, even when he's hard to reach."

Paul nodded. "I won't. I just hope he sees that I'm not trying to be better than him. I just want him to come home."

Samuel, watching Paul's growth with pride, often found himself torn between joy and grief. One son was thriving. The other was slipping. And yet, he knew he couldn't trade one for the other.
Grace, too, remained grounded.
"Paul is a blessing," she said one night. "But he needs us too. Let's not forget to nurture the one who is quietly carrying so much."

Indeed, Paul's achievements were not only trophies for the family—they were testimony. Proof that faith, diligence, and grace could still flourish, even in a house divided by pain.

Samuel and Grace's Struggle to Balance Their Hopes for Both Sons

Samuel and Grace stood each day at the crossroads of pride and pain. On one side was Paul—exceeding expectations, flourishing in his studies, and maturing into a spiritual pillar both at home and in the church. On the other was Peter—once so full of promise, now slipping further into the shadows of rebellion.

Their hearts were stretched in two directions.

"How do you rejoice over one child," Grace asked one night, "without grieving for the other?"

Samuel sat beside her, weary-eyed. "I don't know. I feel guilty every time I celebrate Paul's wins. As if I'm betraying Peter somehow."

They prayed for both sons every night, side by side. Yet even in prayer, the tension was palpable. One child was walking in the light. The other was choosing darkness. And the weight of navigating that contrast without letting it crush either of them—or the boys—was a daily burden.

They tried not to compare, but comparisons whispered in their hearts.

Paul was home before curfew, volunteering at church, mentoring peers. Peter was evasive, dismissive, and often unreachable.

Grace wrestled with silent questions. "Was it something I missed with Peter? Did we push him too hard? Or not hard enough?"

Samuel, on the other hand, often felt as though he had failed to command the kind of authority Peter would respect.

"He sees me as the enemy," Samuel admitted. "And I don't know how to be his father without feeling like his warden."

They tried to shield Paul from their emotional tug-of-war, but he noticed the sorrow behind his mother's smiles and the tension in his father's silence.

One night, after a particularly difficult family argument, Paul approached them.
"I don't want to be the reason you're always sad," he said softly.
"You're not," Grace assured him, pulling him into an embrace. "You're one of the reasons we keep going."
"But I know it's hard to celebrate me when Peter's not okay."

Samuel placed a hand on Paul's shoulder. "Son, your light is not the problem. It's the reminder of what Peter is running from. But don't ever dim it. We need it more than you know."

Despite their efforts, there were moments of imbalance. Times when they lavished attention on Peter, hoping to keep him from falling off the edge, while Paul quietly managed his responsibilities without complaint. Other times, they leaned into Paul's peace, seeking refuge from the emotional drain Peter caused.

"We have to keep seeing both of them through God's eyes," Grace reminded Samuel. "Not just through what they're doing right or wrong, but through who they are becoming."

So they adjusted, again and again. They took turns spending time with each boy, sometimes together, often separately. They celebrated Paul's milestones—his awards, his church involvement, his personal growth—without guilt. And they pursued Peter with relentless love, even when he slammed the door in their faces.

At times, it felt like walking a tightrope in a storm. But Samuel and Grace held each other, held onto faith, and refused to give up on either son.
Because they knew: the same God who was working visibly in Paul's life was still silently weaving redemption into Peter's story.

Peter's Exposure to Harmful Influences

It did not happen all at once. Peter's descent into deeper rebellion was a series of seemingly small compromises—each one pushing him further away from the boy his parents had raised. With every step, the influences around him darkened.

Jamal had introduced him to the group, but it was someone else who led him further into dangerous territory: Malik. Older, sharper, and far more cunning, Malik was the type of person who understood how to manipulate a young man searching for identity.

"Life is a game," Malik said to Peter one day. "You either play it or get played."

Peter was drawn to Malik's confidence. He had money, popularity, and connections. While Jamal acted tough, Malik actually commanded respect—mostly through intimidation, but also through calculated charm. He saw Peter's hunger for validation and exploited it.

"You're smarter than most of the guys I know," Malik told him. "You just need to stop thinking like a church kid."

Peter laughed, pretending the label didn't sting. But inside, something in him twisted.

Soon, Peter was spending time in places he used to avoid. Abandoned parking lots, back alleys, and house parties that pulsed with music and smoke. He was exposed to substances he couldn't even name, conversations laced with profanity and distorted views of masculinity, money, and power.

Grace began noticing the change in his smell, his eyes, his energy.

"Peter," she said one evening, "what are you getting involved in?"

"Nothing," he replied, brushing past her. "You worry too much."

Samuel was more direct. "You come home late, your eyes are red, your clothes reek of smoke. This is not nothing."

Peter snapped. "Maybe if this house didn't feel like a prison, I wouldn't need to breathe somewhere else!"

The words cut deep.

Paul tried to intervene too.

"These guys don't care about you, Peter. They're using you."

"You don't know anything," Peter fired back. "You just sit in your safe little Christian bubble. You think reading the Bible makes you better than me?"

"That's not what I think," Paul said. "But I do know where this path leads. And it's not life."

But Peter wasn't listening anymore. The voices of his new circle were louder—and more exciting. They didn't tell him who to be; they let him choose. Or so it seemed.

The Choices We Make: Seeds of Destiny

Malik began asking favors. At first, they were small—dropping off packages, keeping watch while others handled "business." Peter didn't ask questions. The thrill of being trusted was intoxicating.

"You want respect?" Malik said. "You earn it by doing what others won't."

Eventually, Peter found himself tangled in a web he couldn't easily walk away from. The favors turned into risks. One night, he was nearly caught in a police sweep at a party that was raided for underage drinking and suspected drug trafficking.

He escaped through the back door, heart racing, breath shallow.

That night, he sat on a park bench, staring up at the stars, the weight of his choices pressing on his chest like an iron hand.

"This isn't who I was supposed to be," he muttered to himself.

But even then, pride kept him from turning around.

Back at home, Grace waited in the dark, praying.

Samuel stood by the window, furious and frightened.

And Paul lay awake in his bed, clutching his Bible, whispering Peter's name.

Paul's Growing Sense of Responsibility Within the Church

As Peter delved deeper into destructive choices, Paul leaned harder into the only place that still gave him clarity and peace—the church. The sanctuary became more than a refuge; it became his mission field. In the house of God, Paul felt a responsibility that extended beyond his age. He was no longer just a participant—he was becoming a pillar.

What started as occasional volunteering evolved into active leadership. Brother Mark, recognizing Paul's heart and consistency, began entrusting him with greater roles.

"Paul, I need you to lead the devotional next Friday," he said one evening after Bible study.

Paul blinked. "Me?"

"You've got a voice," Brother Mark smiled. "And more importantly, you've got a walk to back it up."

Paul didn't see himself as a leader. He only saw himself as someone trying to stay faithful. But others began to see what he didn't. His prayers were steady. His insights were thoughtful. His presence was dependable.

Soon, he was leading youth prayer nights, helping with altar calls, and mentoring boys younger than him. Many looked up to him—not because he demanded respect, but because he lived what he believed.

Grace watched with silent gratitude as Paul stood behind the pulpit one Sunday morning to deliver a five-minute word during youth service. He spoke on *"Living Upright in a Crooked World"*—a message that hit even closer to home than he was willing to admit. "You don't have to shout to stand," he said. "You just have to remain when others walk away."

Samuel sat in the congregation, his hands clasped, tears welling in his eyes. His son was becoming everything he had prayed for.

Paul didn't take his growth lightly. He sought counsel regularly, asked questions, and spent hours in personal study. He fasted on Wednesdays, not because he was told to, but because he felt a burden for his generation.

"God," he would pray in his room, "if You can use anyone, use me. Let my life speak louder than my words."

But with increased visibility came increased pressure. People began expecting him to always have it together. To always be spiritual. To always lead.
Paul started to feel the weight.
One evening, he confided in Grace. "What if I mess up? What if I say the wrong thing? What if I'm not enough?"

Grace hugged him. "You don't have to be enough. You just have to be faithful. God does the rest."
Despite his inner struggles, Paul pressed forward. His love for the Word, his commitment to service, and his heart for people kept him grounded. The church became a training ground for leadership, character, and deeper intimacy with God.

And though he often returned home to the chaos of Peter's rebellion, Paul carried into that space a light that could not be quenched.
He knew the path he walked would not be easy. But he had made up his mind to walk it anyway.

Conversations Between Samuel and Grace About Their Sons' Future

The house was quieter at night. Not because peace had returned, but because words had grown tired. There was only so much rebuke, correction, and pleading a parent could give before silence became their language of grief.

It was in that silence that Samuel and Grace often found themselves in hushed conversation—lying in bed long after the lights were out, their hearts too full to sleep.

"He's drifting," Samuel whispered one evening, staring at the ceiling. "I can see the edge, Grace. And Peter is getting closer to it."

Grace turned toward him, her voice soft. "He's not lost. He's wandering. And I'm still believing he'll find his way home."

Samuel sighed deeply. "We raised them the same. How did they become so different?"

"Because they are different. Same roots, different soil. God doesn't raise duplicates. He raises individuals."

There were many nights like this—nights where they replayed every parenting decision, every disciplinary moment, every prayer and missed opportunity.

"Do you think we gave Paul too much attention?" Samuel asked once.
"No," Grace said. "We gave Paul what he needed. And we gave Peter what we thought he needed too. But maybe what Peter needs now is different."
They talked about the future often. About what kind of men their sons would become. About who Paul might marry—"a gentle, praying woman," Grace would smile—and what kind of father he would be. But when it came to Peter, the future felt more like a question mark than a story.

"I'm scared," Samuel admitted one night. "Scared he'll make a mistake he can't recover from. That he'll burn a bridge that can't be rebuilt."
Grace squeezed his hand. "But what if he finds God in the fire? What if the ashes are where he discovers who he really is?"

They considered sending Peter to live with a relative—someone he respected, away from bad influences. They discussed therapy. Disciplinary boarding schools. Even enrolling him in a mentorship program at church.

"We can't force transformation," Grace reminded him. "We can only position him for it."
Samuel nodded. "And keep praying that God will do what we cannot."

They also talked about Paul's burden. How he was silently carrying the weight of the family's grief. How his leadership was blossoming but his heart was heavy.
"He needs to know we see him," Samuel said. "Not just as the obedient son, but as the one quietly bleeding for his brother."
"I'll tell him," Grace replied. "He needs our gratitude too, not just our expectations."
As dawn crept in and their prayers rose with it, they committed again to standing in the gap for both boys.

To hope without giving up. To parent not with perfection, but with perseverance.
"Whatever happens," Grace said, eyes wet with tears, "we will love them both. Through the storm, into the light."
Samuel placed his arm around her shoulders. "Amen."
And so, another day began—with faith a little bruised, but still burning.

The Introduction of Mentors or Negative Influencers for Each Brother

The people we walk with often determine the direction we take. For Peter and Paul, this truth became clearer as their paths continued to diverge—one ascending through godly counsel and spiritual discipline, the other descending through reckless companionship and misguided counsel.

Paul's life was steadily shaped by godly mentors—men and women who saw his potential and poured into him without reservation. Brother Mark remained a central figure, challenging Paul to grow in boldness and wisdom.

"Leadership isn't always about position," he told Paul during one of their mentoring sessions. "It's about posture. You serve your way into influence."
He gave Paul books to read—on character, apologetics, and biblical leadership. They would meet every other Saturday at the church café to talk about life, doctrine, and the pressures of being different.

Sister Naomi also continued her quiet but powerful influence. She guided Paul in prayer, taught him to listen to the Holy Spirit, and shared her own journey of faith with transparency and humor.

"Don't try to impress people," she often told him. "Let your peace speak louder than your performance."

Paul absorbed these lessons like dry ground soaking in rain. He journaled their wisdom, prayed over their counsel, and let it shape not just his public walk, but his private character.

Peter, on the other hand, was being formed in the shadows. His influences didn't wear suits or carry Bibles. They wore chains, wielded street smarts, and spoke in code.

Malik had become more than a bad influence—he had become a voice in Peter's head.
"You've got fire," Malik told him. "But don't waste it trying to please people who don't see you. Use it to get what's yours."

Malik introduced Peter to others—older teens who had been suspended from school multiple times, who made money through shady means, who laughed at prayer and glorified self-preservation.
Peter was drawn in by their confidence, their boldness, their lack of fear. He started echoing their slang, imitating their walk, and internalizing their code.

"If someone disrespects you," one of them said, "you don't turn the other cheek—you show them who's boss."

Grace noticed the shift. His speech had changed. His values seemed distorted. His spiritual appetite was gone.

"He's being discipled," she whispered to Samuel one night. "Just not by the church."

The contrast couldn't have been more painful.
Paul's mentors pointed him to eternity—challenging him to live with purpose, purity, and vision. Peter's influencers pulled him into the present, consumed by status, shortcuts, and survival.

Paul began mentoring a few younger boys in church, not out of pride, but because he had learned from his own mentors the value of investing in others.
Peter, meanwhile, was being groomed to take bigger risks.
One evening, Malik asked him to help "deliver" a package. No questions. No names. Just a time and place.

Peter's hands trembled, but he agreed.

The Choices We Make: Seeds of Destiny

That night, as he passed the package in an alleyway to someone he didn't know, something inside him stirred—a discomfort he hadn't felt in months. It was the last flicker of his conscience, buried but not yet dead.

He walked home faster than usual.

Paul, returning from a church youth vigil that same night, crossed paths with him near the corner.

"Peter," he said, surprised. "Where've you been?"

Peter paused, hiding the nervous shake in his voice. "Out."

"You okay?"

Peter shrugged. "I'm good."

But his eyes told a different story.

Two brothers. Two paths. Two different voices shaping their futures.

And in the unseen realm, heaven and hell watched closely, knowing that mentors, whether righteous or reckless, often hold the pen that helps write a young man's destiny.

Peter's Increasing Resentment Toward Paul's Success

It began with silence—an inward bitterness Peter couldn't explain, a growing discomfort every time Paul received applause, every time their parents smiled with pride at another one of Paul's achievements.

The resentment crept in subtly at first.
Another award at school. Another "thank you" from the youth pastor. Another compliment at the dinner table.
Paul never gloated. He never boasted. But in Peter's eyes, that made it worse. Paul's humility only amplified Peter's feelings of failure. It was like standing in the dark and watching someone else hold the only lamp.

One afternoon, Peter overheard Samuel on a call with a church elder: "Yes, Paul's leading devotion next Sunday again. He's truly a blessing. We thank God."
Peter's chest tightened.

That night, he walked into their shared room and found Paul organizing notes for his next youth message.
"Another sermon?" Peter muttered.
Paul looked up. "Yeah, just something short on the life of Joseph."
Peter scoffed. "Of course. Perfect Paul, the holy preacher."
Paul blinked, confused. "What's that supposed to mean?"
"Nothing," Peter snapped. "It just must be nice to be everyone's favorite."

"Peter, I'm not trying to compete with you—"
"Then stop winning all the time!"
The room fell silent.
Peter stormed out, leaving Paul speechless.

What Peter couldn't voice was the shame he carried. He knew he was drifting. He knew he had made choices that put him at odds with everything their family stood for. And deep down, he hated that Paul kept shining while he struggled in the shadows.

At school, the contrast was just as glaring. Teachers praised Paul while giving Peter concerned looks. At church, people congratulated Paul and asked Grace, in whispered tones, to "keep praying" for Peter.
Peter began to see Paul not as a brother, but as a standard he could never meet.
And that hurt.

One evening, during a family dinner, Grace mentioned that Paul had been nominated for a leadership award at church.
"That's great," she said. "We should all be there to support him."

Peter dropped his fork with a clatter. "Why don't you just take a picture of him and put it on the wall? That way you can all sit around and clap every night!"

"Peter!" Samuel said sharply.
"No, it's fine," Paul said quietly. "I didn't ask for this."
"Exactly," Peter muttered. "You don't have to. Everything just falls into your lap."
That night, Paul found Peter in the garage, sitting alone.
"Look," Paul began, "I don't want your life to feel like it doesn't matter."
Peter didn't look up. "It already does."

Paul sat beside him. "I'm not your enemy, Peter."
"Then stop making me feel like one."
"I'm not trying to make you feel anything. I just… I want you to know you're still loved. Even when you don't see it."
Peter remained silent.

The wedge between them wasn't just about actions—it was about identity. Peter felt invisible in the shadow of Paul's light. And in his heart, envy brewed not because Paul was perfect—but because Paul hadn't fallen.
Resentment turned to distance. Distance into indifference. And yet, beneath the bitterness, Peter longed for something he couldn't admit: the peace Paul seemed to carry.

The Choices We Make: Seeds of Destiny

Chapter Six:

Rising Tensions

Family Conflicts Come to a Head

The Okafor household had always been held together by prayer, tradition, and deep love. But now, those threads were fraying fast. Arguments that once flared occasionally had become daily routines. Cold silences lingered longer than laughter. And beneath the surface of every mealtime, every shared room, every casual glance, was a growing storm.

It was a Sunday evening when the tension finally erupted. Samuel had called for a family meeting—a tradition meant for bonding, reflection, and resolution. But this one felt more like a battlefield than a circle of healing.

Grace, holding her Bible in one hand, opened the meeting with a gentle prayer. Her voice trembled with hope, but the heaviness in the room was unmistakable.

"Let's talk openly tonight," Samuel began, glancing at each of his sons. "No shouting. No walking out. Just the truth."

Peter rolled his eyes but stayed seated. Paul sat stiffly, sensing what was coming.

"Peter," Samuel continued, "this isn't the life we hoped for you. You're not the boy you used to be."

The Choices We Make: Seeds of Destiny

"I'm not a boy anymore," Peter shot back. "That's the problem. You still want me to act like I'm five."
Samuel's tone sharpened. "What I want is for you to respect this home. Your mother. Your brother. Yourself."

Peter laughed bitterly. "Respect? You mean obey without question. Fall in line like Paul the perfect?"
Paul flinched but said nothing.
"That's enough," Grace said softly. "This isn't about Paul. It's about all of us."

Peter stood abruptly. "No, it's always about Paul. You just don't say it. He's the dream, and I'm the disappointment."
"Peter, sit down," Samuel ordered.
"Or what?" Peter challenged. "You'll kick me out? You already did in your heart."
The room went still.

Tears welled in Grace's eyes. "You're our son. Nothing will ever change that."
"Then stop treating me like a failure!" Peter yelled, his voice cracking.
Paul rose, finally speaking. "No one thinks you're a failure, Peter. We just don't know how to reach you anymore."
"I don't need to be reached," Peter snapped. "I need to breathe."

Samuel's voice broke. "You don't see what this is doing to your mother. To this family. You walk around with anger like it's your shield, but it's killing all of us."

Peter's fists clenched. "You want me to change? Maybe look in the mirror first."

He stormed out, slamming the front door behind him. The echo rang through the house like a final verdict.

Grace collapsed into the couch, sobbing. Paul stood frozen. Samuel sank into his chair, his strength spent.

The conflict had reached its boiling point.

And in the silence that followed, the family realized something: this was no longer about winning an argument. It was about saving a son—and holding a family together before it shattered completely.

Paul's Internal Struggle with Balancing Love and Resentment Toward Peter

Paul had always loved his brother. As twins, they had shared a womb, a crib, a childhood full of firsts. But now, that bond felt stretched thin—like a thread pulled too tightly, threatening to snap.

Paul didn't speak of it often. On the outside, he remained composed—serving at church, supporting his parents, maintaining his grades. But on the inside, a battle raged. The more Peter rebelled, the harder it became to hold onto the love that had once come so easily.

There were days when Paul felt angry—deeply, bitterly angry.
Why did Peter get to make all the wrong choices and still demand sympathy? Why did his parents lose sleep over Peter while expecting Paul to keep it together? Why did he feel invisible while his brother's every misstep drew the family's attention? In those moments, Paul would retreat to his room, drop to his knees, and cry out to God.
"Help me not to hate him," he whispered one night. "I don't want to, Lord. But it's hard."

He remembered the way Peter used to make him laugh. The inside jokes. The late-night talks. The dreams they used to share. That Peter seemed like a ghost now—replaced by someone cold, distant, and hostile.
It wasn't just the pain of Peter's words or the chaos he brought to the family. It was the grief of watching someone he loved self-destruct, knowing there was nothing he could do to stop it.

At church, Paul preached about grace. He quoted scriptures about forgiveness. But at home, he often sat in silence, battling thoughts he didn't know how to confess.

One evening, he journaled: *"I love him, but I don't like who he's becoming. And I feel guilty for even thinking that."*

Grace noticed the heaviness in his eyes.

"You're tired," she said gently.

"I'm trying to be okay," Paul replied. "For everyone. But it's hard to carry someone who doesn't want to be helped."

She placed a hand on his. "You're not his savior. Just his brother. Love him—but don't lose yourself trying to rescue him."

Paul nodded slowly. "But if I stop fighting for him, who will?"

He found temporary comfort in scripture:

"Be not overcome of evil, but overcome evil with good." (Romans 12:21)

But the tug-of-war inside him didn't stop. One part of him longed to grab Peter by the collar and shake sense into him. The other part just wanted to pull him into an embrace and cry.

That's what made it so hard.

He couldn't walk away.

But staying hurt too.

So he did the only thing he could: he loved Peter in silence. In prayers. In small acts of kindness Peter never acknowledged. In holding his tongue when the anger boiled. In choosing compassion over revenge.
It wasn't easy.
But it was love.
And for Paul, that was enough to keep trying.

Samuel's Harsh Words and Regrets

Samuel had never been a man of many words. But when he spoke, his voice carried weight. He had built a life on responsibility, resilience, and reverence for God. In his eyes, love meant provision, protection, and discipline. And when those lines were crossed—as Peter crossed them again and again—Samuel responded the only way he knew how: with words that were sharp, stern, and meant to correct.
But lately, even his strongest words felt powerless.
One Saturday afternoon, Peter had come home well past the agreed curfew, reeking of smoke and defiance. Grace had tried to reason with him, but Peter brushed her off and headed toward his room.

Samuel stopped him at the hallway.
"Where have you been?"

"Out," Peter muttered.
"With who? Doing what?"
"Why do you care?" Peter snapped.
And that was it.

Years of fear, frustration, and disappointment boiled over.
"You walk around here like you know everything," Samuel roared. "But all I see is a foolish boy sprinting toward destruction!"
Peter turned slowly, his eyes hard. "Then maybe you should stop looking."
"You think this is strength?" Samuel continued. "You're not strong—you're lost! And if you don't change, you'll end up dead or in prison before your next birthday!"
The words sliced the air like knives.

Peter didn't respond. He stared at Samuel, eyes burning, before walking out and slamming the door behind him.
The silence afterward was deafening.
Grace stood in the kitchen doorway, her face pale.
"Samuel…" she whispered.
But Samuel didn't answer. He sank into the couch, his face in his hands.

He hadn't meant to say it like that. He hadn't meant for his fear to sound like condemnation. But the words were out now—and they echoed louder in his own heart than they ever would in Peter's ears.

Later that night, Samuel sat alone in the living room. The house was quiet. Grace had gone to bed. Paul was upstairs. Peter hadn't returned.
Samuel stared at the framed family photo on the mantel—back when the boys were eight, smiling in matching church outfits, arms wrapped around each other.
"What happened?" he whispered.
He thought about his own father, a man who ruled with an iron voice and a silent hand. Samuel had vowed to do better. To be more present. More kind. But somewhere in the pressure of provision and protection, he had begun speaking more with commands than with compassion.
And now, he feared it was too late.

He bowed his head, tears streaming freely.
"God… I messed up. I've pushed him away. I tried to parent through fear when I should've led with grace."
That night, he wrote a letter. Not one he would give Peter immediately, but one he hoped to share someday.

"Son, I spoke out of fear. Not wisdom. I yelled because I didn't know how to reach you anymore. But the truth is—I love you more than I've ever said. And no matter what you've done or where you go, you're still my son. I'm sorry."

In his harshest moment, Samuel had realized a deeper truth: no amount of shouting could heal what only love could reach.

And in that brokenness, he began to find the courage to speak not from anger—but from the ache of a father who still believed his son could return.

Grace's Attempts at Reconciliation

Grace had never believed in force. Her faith taught her that change, especially the kind that truly lasts, comes not through pressure but through patience, not through argument but through love. And so, even as her family strained under the weight of conflict, she became the quiet bridge—the one still trying to hold the pieces together.

While Samuel's voice thundered with righteous concern and Paul's heart wrestled silently, Grace's approach was different. She chose to listen. She chose to stay close.

She began with small gestures—packing Peter's favorite snacks even when he didn't ask, leaving folded clothes on his bed, gently knocking on his door just to say, "Goodnight."

Peter rarely responded. Sometimes he ignored her entirely. Other times, his answers were clipped and cold.
But she kept showing up.

One afternoon, she found him sitting alone on the back porch, headphones in, hoodie pulled over his head. She walked over and sat beside him in silence. Minutes passed before she finally spoke.
"I remember when you used to tell me everything," she said softly.
Peter didn't respond, but he didn't leave either.
"I don't miss who you used to be," Grace continued. "I miss the closeness. I miss hearing your heart."
He shifted slightly.
"I'm not trying to fix you," she added. "I just want to understand."
That night, she wrote a note and slipped it under his door:

"Peter, I know you feel far, but I believe love still reaches you. I don't need you to be perfect. I just want you to know I haven't stopped praying. And I haven't stopped hoping."

It wasn't a miracle moment. He didn't rush into her arms the next day. But the note was found, read, and tucked quietly into his backpack.

At dinner, she tried including him in conversations, asking questions he could actually answer.

"Did you hear about the new art exhibit downtown?"

He shrugged. "Sort of."

"It looked interesting. I thought of you when I saw the flyer."

Grace didn't expect applause for her effort. She just wanted to keep the lines open. Even if Peter only gave her inches, she took them with gratitude.

With Paul, she reminded him not to harden his heart.

"He's your brother," she said one morning while preparing breakfast. "And brothers don't stop loving when it gets hard. They love more."

She encouraged Samuel, too—softly redirecting him when his frustration threatened to overflow.

"He hears you, even when he doesn't respond. Just make sure what he hears is love."

Grace prayed over Peter's room each morning. She anointed his pillow with oil. She declared scripture aloud when no one was watching.

"The seed of the righteous shall be delivered." (Proverbs 11:21)

She believed Peter was more than the choices he was making. She believed her son still carried destiny, no matter how deep he had buried it.
And so, she reconciled with the idea that reconciliation wouldn't be instant. It would take time. Tenderness. Trust.

But she also believed in miracles.
And she believed that sometimes, the greatest miracle was a heart that dared to keep loving—even when it had every reason to walk away.

Peter's Destructive Behaviors Intensify
What had once been subtle acts of rebellion—late nights, skipped classes, missed devotions—soon gave way to something darker, more alarming. Peter's behavior no longer just strained the home; it started to shake its foundation.

He began disappearing for days at a time, returning only to shower, grab clean clothes, and vanish again without explanation. His eyes looked heavier, more guarded. His words sharper, and his silences longer. The boy who once sang in the children's choir had become a stranger under their roof.
It started with another incident at school.

Peter was caught in a violent confrontation with another student. Rumors spread that it wasn't just a fight—it was retaliation. There had been whispers of stolen items, and the administration was forced to suspend him pending further investigation.

Samuel and Grace were called in for a meeting.

"Your son is extremely intelligent," the vice-principal said. "But he's heading toward something dangerous if this continues. We've tried warnings, detentions, counselling referrals. Nothing seems to stick."

Samuel sat in silence, rage and shame boiling beneath his calm exterior. Grace could only nod, clutching her purse like a lifeline.

When they returned home, Peter showed no remorse.

"They started it," he muttered. "I finished it."

"That's not strength," Samuel barked. "That's recklessness!"

Peter shrugged. "Then maybe I'm reckless."

The house became tense with constant confrontation. Peter began coming home smelling of alcohol. There were strange phone calls late into the night—coded words and muffled laughter. One evening, Paul found a small bag of pills hidden under Peter's mattress.

He didn't confront him directly. He gave it to Samuel.

Samuel didn't speak for hours. When Peter returned home that night, his father stood at the door, silent and pale.
"You bring drugs into this house?" he asked quietly.
Peter met his gaze without flinching. "It's not like I'm selling them."
"You think that makes it better?"
"Maybe I don't care anymore," Peter said, walking past.

Samuel didn't sleep that night.
Grace cried in the kitchen until dawn.
Paul sat outside Peter's door, whispering prayers through clenched teeth.
And then came the arrest.

It was a Friday evening when the doorbell rang. Two police officers stood on the porch. Peter had been picked up with a group of older boys involved in a vandalism spree at a local shopping center. Graffiti, broken windows, theft.
Samuel's hands trembled as he signed the release papers.

Peter didn't speak during the car ride home.
That night, the family sat in stunned silence.

"How did we get here?" Grace whispered.
"I don't know," Samuel replied. "But we're losing him."
Peter, sitting in the darkness of his room, stared at the ceiling.

He didn't know how to stop anymore. He didn't know how to turn around.
Every bad decision pulled him deeper into a world that made fewer demands but exacted greater costs. And though he didn't admit it, he missed the days when life was simpler, when he felt whole, when he still believed he was more than the pain he now caused.
But the spiral had begun.
And he wasn't sure how to escape it.

Paul's Journey Toward Becoming a Youth Leader

While Peter spiraled deeper into rebellion, Paul's quiet ascent in character and influence continued within the church. The turbulence at home didn't hinder his commitment—it refined it. The more brokenness he saw around him, the more determined he became to be a vessel of healing and hope.
Brother Mark took notice early on.

"You have the spirit of a shepherd, Paul," he said after one youth Bible study. "Not just someone who teaches, but someone who leads with love."

Paul didn't know what to say. He didn't feel worthy of the title 'leader.' He still battled doubts, still wrestled with silent pain over Peter. But something inside him stirred. Maybe God was raising him not because he was perfect, but because he was willing.

Brother Mark began mentoring him more intentionally—walking Paul through the Scriptures, teaching him about servant leadership, spiritual authority, and the importance of integrity.
"You don't lead from a stage," he told him. "You lead from your knees."

Paul took those words to heart.
He began to lead small prayer sessions before youth meetings. He was entrusted with organizing Bible study groups and planning worship nights. His consistency, his humility, and his quiet depth made him a role model for younger teens.
One evening, during a regional youth conference, the host pastor invited Paul to speak for ten minutes. His topic: *Faithfulness in the Fire*.
He stood nervously at the podium, gripping his notes. But as he looked around at the young faces, something unlocked inside him.

"I used to think being a leader meant being perfect," he said. "But I've learned that God uses us in our weakness. He calls us even when our lives are messy. Even when we're hurting."

The room was silent. A few heads nodded. Some wiped tears.

That night marked a shift. Paul wasn't just helping the youth ministry—he was becoming one of its voices.

Grace and Samuel watched with quiet pride. For all the pain they carried over Peter, Paul's walk reminded them that their labor was not in vain.

"He's an old soul," Grace whispered once to Samuel after one of Paul's teachings.

"No," Samuel replied with a rare smile. "He's an anointed one."

But even as Paul stepped into leadership, he remained grounded. He often stayed late after youth meetings to clean up. He called struggling teens during the week to pray with them. He fasted for wisdom and clarity.

And still, every night, he prayed for Peter.

"God, if You're raising me up, don't leave him behind."

Becoming a youth leader wasn't a title for Paul—it was a calling. A calling that grew not from the absence of struggle, but from his resolve to walk in the light, even while his brother stumbled through the dark.

A Significant Event That Widens the Rift Between the Brothers

It was supposed to be a day of celebration. The church had organized its annual youth conference, and Paul had been selected to deliver the keynote message—an honor typically reserved for older leaders. It was a culmination of years of quiet service, spiritual discipline, and unwavering commitment. For Paul, it felt like the beginning of something greater.
But for Peter, it felt like the final insult.

The night before the event, Grace had gently encouraged Peter to attend.
"It would mean a lot to Paul," she said. "Just come and sit. You don't even have to stay long."
Peter shrugged. "Church people don't want me there. They just want their golden boy."
"Peter," Grace said softly, "your presence is your support. Not for the crowd—for your brother."
He didn't answer.

The next morning, the sanctuary buzzed with energy. Teens and youth leaders from across the city filled the pews. Paul stood backstage, his heart pounding, his message clutched tightly in trembling hands. When he peeked through the curtain, he searched for one face—his brother's. It wasn't there.

Still, he took the stage.

He spoke with power and clarity, drawing from the story of Moses—how God used even a man with a past to deliver a people into freedom. The crowd responded with standing ovations and tearful prayers.

Paul stepped down to thunderous applause.

That evening, as the family returned home, Paul found Peter in the garage, seated with his hood over his head, earphones blaring.

"You didn't come," Paul said quietly.

Peter looked up. "Didn't need to."

"It wasn't about the church. It was about us."

Peter scoffed. "You're doing fine without me."

"That's not true."

Peter stood up, eyes flashing. "You think I want to sit there and watch everyone worship you? Watch them act like you're some saint while they side-eye me like I'm the family disgrace?"

"No one thinks that."

"Yes, they do!" Peter shouted. "And maybe they're right!"

The words stung. Paul stepped back.
"I didn't ask for any of this," he said. "All I ever wanted was for us to walk this path together."
Peter shook his head. "You never needed me, Paul. You left me behind a long time ago."
"No," Paul replied, voice trembling, "you're the one who left."
There was no yelling after that. Just a cold silence. And in that silence, something shifted. A wall that had once been fragile became firm, fortified by years of pain and pride.
From that day forward, Peter stopped acknowledging Paul's efforts. He refused to attend family dinners if Paul was leading prayer. He skipped church altogether. He cut off even the small moments of brotherhood that had once remained.
The rift was no longer subtle. It was wide. Obvious. Painful.

And for the first time, Paul didn't chase him.
He still prayed. Still loved. But he no longer forced the bond.
Because sometimes, healing takes space.
And sometimes, the crack must fully open before grace can begin to fill it.

Samuel's Health Beginning to Fail Under Stress

Samuel had always carried the weight of his family like a seasoned warrior. Every bill paid, every crisis managed, every prayer whispered late into the night—all of it had rested squarely on his shoulders. But those shoulders were beginning to tremble.

At first, it was just fatigue—longer naps after work, heavier sighs, the occasional wince as he climbed the stairs. Grace noticed the change before he did.

"You're not as strong as you used to be," she said softly one evening.

"I'm just tired," Samuel replied, brushing her concern aside. "It's nothing."

But it was something.

The constant tension in the house, the repeated confrontations with Peter, the disappointment, the helplessness—each day it chipped away at his peace, until even his body began to signal surrender.

One morning, Samuel collapsed in the kitchen.

Grace screamed his name, rushing to his side. Paul called the ambulance, his hands shaking as he tried to stay calm. Peter stood frozen in the doorway, guilt flashing across his face.

At the hospital, doctors ran tests and delivered the sobering news: Samuel had dangerously high blood pressure and was at risk of heart failure if he didn't slow down.
"He needs rest. He needs emotional relief," the doctor said. "Stress like this will only make things worse."

Grace stayed by Samuel's bedside, her fingers intertwined with his.
"I'm sorry," he whispered, tears pooling in his eyes. "I've tried to hold this family together with my strength. But I've run out."
"You don't need to be strong all the time," Grace replied gently. "You just need to be here."

The sight of Samuel, frail and worn, shook the family. Paul took on even more responsibilities at home. He became the man of the house in a deeper way—not with authority, but with care.
Peter visited once. Just once.

He stood awkwardly at the edge of the hospital room, staring at the wires and monitors. For a brief moment, he saw his father not as the towering figure of discipline, but as a man who had given everything—and was breaking because of it.
Samuel opened his eyes and saw him.
"Peter," he said, his voice weak.

Peter stepped closer, silent.

"I don't care what you've done," Samuel murmured. "You're still my son. I'm still praying for you."

Peter blinked fast. "I didn't ask for your prayers."

"But you need them."

He turned and walked away, but something in his step was different. Slower. Heavier.

Samuel's illness didn't heal the brokenness overnight, but it did reveal something powerful: even the strongest can fall. And when they do, what holds a family together isn't control—it's compassion.

Chapter Seven:

A Divergence of Paths

Paul's Academic Success and Spiritual Growth

With Samuel recovering and the family walking the fragile line between healing and heartbreak, Paul began to emerge as a beacon of hope and strength. His diligence, once viewed as admirable, now became essential. While the foundation of the family was under stress, Paul's consistency was the glue holding it all together.

In school, Paul's academic performance reached new heights. He received an invitation to apply for a prestigious leadership scholarship reserved for students with outstanding academic records and community involvement. His teachers praised his essays, his research projects, and his ability to lead classroom discussions with humility and intelligence.

"Paul is not just book-smart," one teacher noted. "He's thoughtful. Compassionate. The kind of young man every parent prays to raise."

But Paul didn't let the accolades change him. His identity was not rooted in grades or applause—it was grounded in something deeper: his relationship with God.

His morning devotions became sacred. Before the sun rose, Paul could be found in the corner of the living room, Bible open, journal in hand, whispering prayers over his family.

"Lord, give me wisdom beyond my age," he often prayed. "And give me grace to keep loving when it's hardest."

At church, he became a recognized youth leader—officially commissioned by the pastor after consistent service and a growing reputation for integrity. He led Bible studies, mentored younger teens, and even helped plan the upcoming youth retreat.
But Paul's spiritual growth wasn't just seen in public. It was lived in private.

He prayed over his father's hospital bed. He encouraged Grace in moments of fatigue. He left anonymous Bible verses taped to Peter's door.

"The light shineth in darkness; and the darkness comprehended it not." (John 1:5)

Paul didn't know if Peter read them. But he left them anyway.

His spiritual maturity was forged not just in church pews, but in the tension of unanswered prayers, in the weight of unspoken grief. While others saw a strong young man, Paul knew he was only standing because of grace.

He began considering ministry more seriously—not necessarily as a profession, but as a lifestyle.
"Wherever I end up," he told Brother Mark, "I want to serve people. I want my life to point to something greater than me."
Brother Mark smiled. "Then you're already in ministry."

At school, he was chosen to deliver the valedictory address for his graduating class. At church, he was asked to represent the youth during the Easter celebration. Everywhere he turned, God was opening doors.

But through it all, Paul's heart remained burdened for one thing—Peter.
Because no matter how high he soared, he never stopped looking over his shoulder for the brother who once walked beside him.

Peter's Increasing Detachment from Family and Faith

Peter's descent wasn't marked by loud rebellion anymore—it had evolved into something quieter, colder. Detachment became his language. He wasn't just pulling away from church or school. He was drifting entirely—from family, from faith, from anything that had once anchored him.
Grace noticed it in the little things first.

He stopped showing up for dinner. The sound of his footsteps around the house became scarce. The light in his room stayed on until dawn and was off during daylight. Conversations were reduced to nods or shrugs. Even eye contact became rare.

The Bible that once sat on his shelf was gone. His room no longer held even a trace of the boy who used to memorize verses with Paul or sing quietly during family devotions. The crucifix that used to hang on his wall now lay buried in the bottom of a drawer.

Grace knocked one evening, holding a plate of food. "Peter?"

"I'm not hungry," came the muffled reply.

She lingered at the door. "Can I pray with you?"

"No."

He didn't say it with anger, just emptiness.

The church had become a place he avoided completely. Youth leaders called and texted, but he never responded. On Sundays, while the rest of the family dressed for service, Peter would slip out through the back door and vanish for hours.

Samuel, still recovering, said little about it. But the pain in his eyes was unmistakable.

"I failed him," he whispered to Grace. "I drove him too hard. Now he's running from everything we gave him."

Grace gently disagreed. "He's not running from us. He's running from what he believes no longer has answers."

Paul, too, felt the distance. He tried reaching out in subtle ways—leaving notes, starting light conversations—but Peter made it clear: the bridge was burned.

"You don't get it," Peter said one night when Paul knocked on his door.

"Then help me understand."

"There's nothing to understand. I don't fit here. I don't fit there. I just want to disappear."

Those words haunted Paul.

Peter spent more time with people whose lives reflected chaos. Friends who laughed at God, mocked discipline, and found power in isolation. He wasn't necessarily happy in their company—but he felt less judged, less seen.

He started talking about moving out, dropping out, cutting off everything familiar. The idea of freedom—raw, unfiltered, and unbound—had taken root.

"Church is fake," he said one evening to a friend. "God's not real. And if He is, He stopped listening a long time ago."

But in his most silent, sleepless moments, when even his music couldn't drown out the ache, Peter still remembered the sound of his mother's voice praying, the warmth of his brother's laughter, the way Samuel once called him "champ."
He remembered—but refused to return.

His heart had grown numb. His spirit, once curious and tender, was now calloused by disappointment, anger, and shame.
Peter was not just lost.
He was hiding.
And no one knew exactly how to bring him back.

Grace's Heartbreak and Persistence in Prayer
Grace had learned over the years that heartbreak wasn't always loud. Sometimes, it was a slow ache—a quiet grief that settled into your bones and refused to leave. Watching Peter drift further away from the boy she once rocked to sleep, the son she taught to fold his hands in prayer, tore at her soul in ways words could never express.

Every door slam, every missed dinner, every unanswered call from the church reminded her that she was fighting a war she could not see, against an enemy she could not touch. But what she could do—what she knew how to do—was pray.
And she did.

Night after night, long after everyone had gone to bed, Grace remained on her knees in the living room. Sometimes with tears. Sometimes in silence. Sometimes with nothing more than a whisper: "Lord, don't let go of my son."

She prayed over Peter's room when he was gone. She anointed his pillow with oil, laid hands on his shoes, and slipped scriptures into the pockets of his jackets.
One of her favorite verses was Isaiah 49:25:
"For I will contend with him that contendeth with thee, and I will save thy children."

She repeated it like a mantra.
Grace didn't pretend to have it all together. There were moments when the pain felt unbearable. When she saw Paul flourishing while Peter unraveled, guilt gnawed at her. "What did I do differently?" she would ask herself. "Did I miss something?"
Samuel tried to comfort her, though his body was still recovering and his own heart was heavy. "You didn't fail him," he told her. "You're the reason he's still breathing grace."

But the mother in her couldn't be convinced easily. Still, she pressed on.

She kept attending every church service, even when her heart was raw. She smiled through the questions and the pitying looks. She worshipped with tears on her cheeks and hope in her voice.

She never stopped setting Peter's place at the dinner table.

She never stopped saying "Goodnight" at his door, even when she knew he wasn't listening.

One night, she wrote him a letter she never planned to send:

"I don't need you to be perfect, Peter. I just need you to remember who you are. No matter where you go, I will never stop believing in the boy who used to pray beside me. I will love you until the day my breath runs out—and even then, my prayers will still be echoing in heaven."

Her heartbreak didn't harden her.

It made her more tender, more resolute. Her prayers weren't filled with desperation—they were declarations of faith.

"God," she said one evening, "even if it takes years. Even if I don't see it. Let him find his way back to You. Let him know he's still loved. Still chosen. Still Yours."

Because Grace believed what she had always believed:

That God doesn't lose children.

Even when they wander, even when they forget, even when they break everything in sight—He still knows how to bring prodigals home.

Samuel's Frustration Turning Into Resignation

Samuel had once been the thunder in the household—the voice of command, of clarity, of conviction. He spoke with certainty, led with discipline, and raised his sons with a clear sense of right and wrong. But over the years, as Peter drifted deeper into rebellion and silence became his most frequent answer, Samuel found that the thunder in him had quieted.

What began as righteous frustration slowly gave way to something more painful: resignation.
He still loved his son, of course. But love had become a silent burden rather than a joyful expression. He had said everything he knew to say. Prayed every prayer he could muster. Watched Grace carry the emotional weight with steadfast gentleness. Watched Paul mature with grace beyond his years. And yet, Peter remained distant.

One morning, as he watched Paul leave for school and Peter disappear without a word, Samuel exhaled a long, heavy breath.

"I don't know what else to do," he told Grace. "I feel like I'm trying to hold onto someone who doesn't want to be held."

Grace, ever hopeful, reached for his hand. "You don't have to hold him. Just don't stop believing in him."

But belief was beginning to feel like naivety.

In his quiet moments, Samuel questioned everything. Had he been too harsh? Too firm? Had he mistaken fear for discipline? He remembered his own father—unforgiving and stoic—and feared he had replicated the same patterns in the name of responsibility.

He began to speak less. He stopped checking Peter's room late at night. He no longer confronted him at the door. The fire in his tone faded to embers.

One evening, after a particularly tense silence at dinner, Paul approached him.

"Dad, don't give up on him," he said. "He's still watching. Even when he acts like he doesn't care."

Samuel nodded slowly, eyes distant. "I'm not giving up. I'm just tired of hoping."

"Then let me hope for both of us," Paul replied.

Samuel looked at his son and felt both pride and sorrow. He had wanted to be the one to pass on wisdom, to guide Peter and Paul both into manhood.

But now, it seemed Paul had taken the torch while Peter wandered in the dark.

"I've become a father to one," Samuel murmured to himself, "and a stranger to the other."

Even in church, Samuel became quieter. He no longer offered advice at men's fellowship meetings. He sat in the back row, his prayers fewer but deeper.

"Lord," he said one Sunday, "if I was wrong in how I led him, forgive me. But please… don't let this story end in pain."

Samuel's resignation wasn't hopelessness. It was weariness. A soul tired from years of striving to fix what only God could mend.

But even in resignation, a flicker remained.

A small, tired, faithful flame.

Because sometimes, the strongest kind of faith is the one that stays even when it no longer knows what to say.

Paul's First Encounter with Love and Romantic Relationships

Love was not something Paul was looking for—not consciously, at least. His focus had always been his faith, his academics, and the fragile unity of his home. With so much weight already on his shoulders, romance felt like a distant luxury, reserved for people whose lives were simpler.
And yet, there she was.

Her name was Naomi—a fellow youth leader from a neighboring church, introduced during a collaborative Bible study weekend. She wasn't loud or flashy. She had a calm presence, a kind voice, and eyes that seemed to really see people. For Paul, their first conversation was like breathing fresh air.
They discussed scripture, community outreach, and the challenges of growing up in faith while surrounded by chaos. Naomi understood things Paul never had to explain. She, too, had a sibling who had wandered. She, too, knew what it was to pray in silence, to carry others' burdens while managing her own.

They started slow—texts after church events, short calls to check in. Their friendship bloomed with ease, grounded in mutual respect and spiritual sincerity.

But friendship began to give way to something more.

One Sunday afternoon, after a youth rally, they took a walk in the park. The conversation drifted from ministry and music to dreams and fears. Paul found himself opening up about Peter, about the weight he carried, about the doubt that sometimes crept into his faith.

Naomi listened without judgment.

"You're strong," she said, "but even strong people need someone to lean on."

He didn't know what to say, but her words stayed with him.

It wasn't long before Paul approached Brother Mark.

"I think I'm developing feelings," he said. "And I don't want to be distracted."

Brother Mark smiled. "Son, love isn't a distraction when it's healthy. It can be a gift—if it's rooted in purpose and peace."

With prayer and counsel, Paul and Naomi began courting—a word they both cherished for its intentionality. They set boundaries. They invited spiritual mentors into their journey. They kept Christ at the center.

Paul found new joy in his days. Naomi's presence brought laughter, encouragement, and a sense of shared calling. For the first time in a long while, he didn't feel alone in his walk.

Grace and Samuel noticed the change. More smiles. More balance. More light in his eyes.

"She's good for him," Grace said quietly one evening.

"God sent her," Samuel replied.

Still, Paul was careful not to idolize the relationship. He continued leading, serving, and praying. But now, there was someone cheering him on, someone praying alongside him—not just for Peter, but for their own shared future.

And though he didn't talk about it much, in the quiet corners of his heart, Paul began to hope.

Hope not just for Peter.

But for himself.

Peter's Own Relationship Entanglements and Poor Decisions

While Paul's journey into love was marked by intention, prayer, and clarity, Peter's foray into relationships was clouded by confusion, brokenness, and unmet needs. What Paul approached as a sacred bond, Peter treated as a temporary escape—a distraction from the ache of a life that felt directionless.

Her name was Lacey. They met through mutual friends at a late-night house party. She was bold, impulsive, and lived by the motto "no rules, no regrets." For Peter, that attitude was magnetic. It mirrored the emotional chaos he was trying to normalize within himself.

Lacey didn't ask about his past. She didn't care where he went or what he believed. She made him feel wanted, even if only for shallow reasons. And at that time, feeling wanted—even superficially—was enough.

The relationship moved quickly. Late-night texts turned into weekend sleepovers. They drank, experimented, and laughed loudly in public while fighting viciously in private. It wasn't love—it was survival dressed as intimacy.

Peter ignored the warning signs. The jealous outbursts. The manipulation. The lies. Part of him even welcomed the drama. It made him feel something, anything, in a life that had grown numb. Grace suspected something was wrong. Peter came home later than ever. Some mornings he didn't come home at all. His temper was shorter. His moods darker.

"Who are you becoming, Peter?" she asked gently one day.

He did not answer.

Samuel tried to confront him but was met with a wall of silence.
Then came the pregnancy scare.
Peter sat on the edge of his bed, phone in hand, as Lacey cried on the other end. "I might be pregnant," she whispered.

Panic gripped him like never before. Not because of the potential child—but because he knew he was in no place to lead a life, let alone raise one.
The test turned out negative, but the moment shook him.

Still, it wasn't enough to make him change.
Instead of pulling away, he clung to Lacey even tighter. She became his crutch, and he became hers. They spiraled together—attending fewer classes, skipping work, ignoring calls from anyone who cared.

When she eventually broke things off—citing "too much baggage"—Peter didn't argue.
He just walked away.
That night, he returned home and sat in the hallway, back against the wall, head in his hands. Grace passed him by, paused, and gently placed her hand on his shoulder.

"I still believe in you," she whispered.
He didn't respond.

The pain of rejection piled onto an already heavy soul. And instead of turning back, Peter slipped deeper into isolation. He convinced himself that love wasn't real. That commitment was a trap. That people only stay until it costs them too much.

Unlike Paul, Peter had never known what it meant to build something sacred with another. He had only known what it felt like to grasp at comfort, to chase adrenaline, to try and fill an inner void with temporary pleasure.
But none of it worked.
He was lonelier than ever.

Attempts at Reconciliation That Only Deepen the Divide

Hope is a fragile thing. And in the Okafor home, hope had taken many forms—silent prayers, handwritten notes, lingering hugs, and conversations that began with trembling words. Everyone, in their own way, had tried to reach Peter.

But the attempts at reconciliation, though born from love, often landed like arrows instead of olive branches.

The Choices We Make: Seeds of Destiny

The first came from Paul.
He had just returned from a youth leadership retreat, his heart full of renewed vision and a sermon about forgiveness still echoing in his ears. He walked into Peter's room one evening, uninvited but determined.
"Can we talk?"
Peter barely looked up. "About what?"
"I don't want us to keep living like enemies."
"We're not enemies," Peter said coldly. "We're just different. You go to church. I go to parties. Let it be."
"I want to understand," Paul said. "I miss us."
"Then you're the only one who does."
Paul left that night feeling more distant from his brother than ever before.

The second attempt came from Grace.
She planned a quiet dinner. Just the four of them. No lectures, no questions. Just food and presence. She cooked Peter's favorite dish, set the table with care, and asked everyone to come with open hearts.
Peter arrived an hour late.
The food was cold. The silence was heavy.
When Grace gently offered him a plate, he sighed and pushed it aside. "This doesn't fix anything, Mom."
"We're not trying to fix everything tonight," she said. "We just want you here."

Peter stood up. "You want me quiet and obedient. I'm not that guy anymore."
He left before dessert.

Samuel tried as well. After weeks of praying and reflecting, he knocked on Peter's door late one night.
"I owe you an apology," he began.
Peter raised an eyebrow. "For what?"
"For trying to shape you through fear. For leading more with rules than with grace."
Peter didn't speak for a long time. Then he said, "Thanks… but I don't think it matters now."
Samuel's heart sank.

Each attempt, sincere as it was, seemed to reinforce to Peter how far he had fallen—and how unlikely it felt that he could ever return.
He began avoiding home more than ever. The house no longer felt like a battleground—it felt like a reminder of everything he'd broken and could never repair.
In their efforts to bring him back, the family unknowingly highlighted how lost he was. And Peter, rather than receive their love, internalized it as pity.
"I don't need fixing," he muttered to himself one night. "I just need space."

And so, reconciliation—so deeply desired—became another wedge.
Not because it was wrong.
But because timing, trust, and tenderness must dance together for healing to begin.

Peter's Decision to Leave Home or Take a Destructive Path

Peter had always flirted with the edge—testing boundaries, pushing limits, living recklessly just close enough to danger without falling completely. But now, that edge felt more like a doorway, and for the first time, he was seriously considering stepping through it.

His relationships had crumbled. Trust in his family had been severed. His reputation in school was ruined. And worse, he had lost his grip on who he was.

The house had grown unbearably quiet around him. Grace no longer knocked as often. Samuel no longer corrected him. Paul no longer tried to start conversations. It was as though the world around him had finally stopped trying, and that, somehow, hurt more than the yelling ever did.

One evening, he stood at the front door with a backpack in his hand. Inside were a few clothes, his phone, some money he'd scraped together, and a half-empty bottle of pills he didn't remember buying.
He didn't say goodbye.
He just walked out.
The air outside felt different—heavy, uncertain. But it carried the illusion of freedom.

Peter ended up crashing on couches, staying with friends who didn't ask too many questions. He started partying harder, drinking more, experimenting with substances that numbed both his guilt and his pain.
There were nights he didn't remember.
Mornings he didn't want to.

At first, it felt like freedom. No curfews, no sermons, no disapproving glances. But quickly, it turned into something else. Loneliness. Emptiness. Chaos.

One night, after a party spiraled into violence and someone pulled a knife, Peter ran until his legs gave out. He collapsed on a park bench, sweat-drenched and shaking, the weight of his choices finally crashing in.

He pulled out his phone and stared at the screen.
No messages.
No missed calls.
No one was looking for him anymore.
And that was the moment.

The moment he realized he had made a choice—not just to leave home, but to walk a path that could very well lead to his destruction.
He didn't cry.
He didn't pray.
He just sat in the dark, alone.

Back home, Grace stood at his empty room, whispering his name in prayer. Samuel lay awake, eyes open, waiting for a door that wouldn't open. Paul stared out his window, torn between anger and heartbreak.
Peter had made his choice.
And the road ahead would demand everything.

Chapter Eight:

The Breaking Point

A Devastating Fallout between Peter and Paul

It wasn't planned. It wasn't staged. But it had been building for years—the tension, the misunderstanding, the hurt. And when the fallout came, it shattered what little was left of the fragile bridge between Peter and Paul.

Peter had been gone for days, living on the edge with people who had no stake in his future. He was spiraling—faster, deeper, more recklessly than ever before. Drugs, fights, stolen moments in strange rooms. He didn't care anymore. Or so he told himself.

But something brought him back that night.
A bruise on his face, a busted lip, and the realization that even the people he was running with had limits—and he had crossed one.
He came home unannounced, pushing the front door open just after midnight. Grace gasped when she saw him. Paul stood up from the couch, stunned.
"Peter?" Grace whispered, rushing to his side.
He winced. "I'm fine."
"No, you're not," she said, guiding him to sit.

Paul stood nearby, fists clenched. His heart broke at the sight of his brother—but the fury inside him boiled hotter.

"Why now?" Paul asked. "Why show up now, when everyone's nearly given up?"

Peter didn't answer.

Grace tried to speak, but Paul raised a hand. "No, Mom. He's not going to walk in and pretend like nothing happened."

Peter glared. "I didn't come for a sermon."

"Then why did you come?"

"To rest. To breathe. Is that a crime now?"

Paul stepped closer. "You don't get to tear this family apart, vanish for weeks, and then stroll in like a victim."

Peter stood up, his face twisted with rage. "You think you're better than me because you pray? Because you speak in church? You don't know half of what I've been through."

"I know I stayed," Paul shot back. "I know I fought while you ran. I know I picked up the pieces you left behind."

Peter shoved him. "Then keep them. I never asked you to fix anything."

Paul shoved him back. "And I never asked you to destroy everything."

Samuel appeared in the hallway, his weak voice rising. "Enough."
But it was too late.

Peter stormed out again. This time not to a friend's place—but into the streets, into the cold, into the darkness he had grown too familiar with.
Grace collapsed into Samuel's arms, weeping.
Paul stared at the door, his chest heaving, guilt mixing with frustration.
This was it.

The moment when years of buried pain erupted.
And in that eruption, both brothers were left wounded—not just by each other's words, but by the realization that love alone hadn't been enough to hold them together.

Samuel and Grace's Heartbreak as Their Sons' Paths Fully Diverge

Samuel and Grace sat in the quiet aftermath, their hearts hollow, their hope stretched thin. The house no longer rang with laughter or argument—it throbbed with silence. A silence that spoke of the distance that had finally, painfully, become undeniable.

Peter had not returned since the confrontation. No calls. No messages. No footsteps down the hall. It was as if he had vanished into the very darkness they had prayed he would escape. And though Paul remained, strong and steadfast, his presence was a reminder of what could have been—a mirror of faith and obedience that only deepened the ache of the one who had strayed.

Grace moved through the house like a woman in mourning. She cooked Peter's favorite meals, placed them on the table, and quietly returned them to the fridge untouched. She kept his room clean, fluffed his pillow, left the door slightly ajar every night.
"Just in case," she whispered.

Samuel, once the voice of command, had grown quieter than ever. He spent long hours sitting in Peter's empty room, eyes closed, recalling memories that now felt like dreams—the boys' first day of school, family prayers, Sunday lunches filled with laughter.
"I thought we did everything right," he said one evening.
Grace sat beside him, tears welling. "Maybe we did. Maybe it's just… the world got louder than we did."
They wept together that night—not for the mistakes they made, but for the distance they couldn't undo.

For the son who once clung to their hands but now walked a road they couldn't follow.

And yet, amid the heartbreak, they clung to something else.

Faith.

They prayed—not with the fiery confidence of the past, but with the quiet desperation of those who had lost nearly everything but dared to believe in restoration.

"Lord," Samuel prayed one night, voice cracking, "we gave them everything. Please don't let it be in vain."

Grace added through tears, "Bring him back, even if we never see it. Let him know You still love him… and so do we."

Their sons had diverged. One on the path of purpose. The other wandering in pain.

And in the chasm between them, Samuel and Grace stood like wounded sentinels—watching, waiting, praying.

Because even when the road splits wide and love is tested beyond its limits, the heart of a parent refuses to stop believing.

The Choices We Make: Seeds of DESTINY

The Consequences of Peter's Choices Becoming Evident

It started slowly, like cracks spidering across a glass window—barely noticeable at first, but irreversible once they spread. The choices Peter had made over the months—choices born out of pain, anger, and confusion—began to reveal their weight.

The first sign came in the form of a letter. A school expulsion notice. Peter had been caught in possession of illegal substances on school property. It wasn't his first offense, and the administration had run out of patience.

Samuel read the letter in silence, his hands trembling. Grace sat beside him, weeping.
Paul clenched his jaw, staring at the paper. "I warned him," he muttered. "I told him this would happen."
The second came through a phone call—Peter had been involved in a police investigation linked to a theft. Though not charged, his name had surfaced as someone "of interest."

He stopped coming home entirely.
Word spread fast in the community. Church members offered condolences masked as conversations. Teachers who once saw promise in

him spoke with disappointment. The name Peter Okafor, once whispered with admiration, now drew raised eyebrows and silent sighs.

Even his so-called friends began to pull away. The same crowd that had cheered him on at parties now distanced themselves, unwilling to share in the consequences.

Peter began couch-surfing, picking up odd jobs under the table, and avoiding any setting that reminded him of who he once was.

But the consequences were no longer external.
They were internal.
He had lost trust.
Lost direction.
Lost peace.

And now, the weight of it all pressed on his chest like a boulder. There were nights he stared at the ceiling in unfamiliar rooms, wondering how he'd gone from singing worship songs at home to stealing to survive.

His reflection became a stranger.
His silence grew heavier.
The boy who once dreamed of becoming a lawyer or teacher now drifted through life without anchor or aim.

The Choices We Make: Seeds of Destiny

And yet, deep inside the wreckage, a flicker remained—a distant echo of the prayers his mother once whispered, the words his father once spoke, the warmth of his brother's hand.

But for now, Peter bore the full weight of his decisions.

And the cost was higher than he ever imagined.

Paul's Struggle to Forgive and Remain Steadfast

Paul had always believed forgiveness was a pillar of faith. He had preached it, taught it to others, and quoted scriptures that urged believers to let go of bitterness. But when it came to Peter—his own brother, his own blood—those teachings became much harder to live out.

Peter had hurt him. Repeatedly.

Not just with words or rebellion, but with absence—missing birthdays, ignoring calls, showing up only to ignite chaos and leaving again just as quickly. Paul had watched their parents weep, had cleaned up the emotional debris left behind after every one of Peter's departures, and had tried—time and again—to be the brother who still believed.

But belief was tiring.

And now, with Peter's consequences rippling through their family—expulsion, legal threats, whispered rumors—Paul found himself battling something deeper: resentment.

He didn't want to hate his brother. But there were moments when he wondered what his life would be like if Peter had never come back that night. If he had stayed gone.

"Lord," he prayed late one evening, "how do I forgive someone who keeps reopening the same wound?"

He thought of the parable of the prodigal son. He wanted to be like the father in that story. He really did. But some days, he felt more like the older brother—watching, hurting, feeling forgotten.

At church, Paul's ministry never wavered. He still preached, still led the youth group, still counseled others through their pain. But inside, he felt like a hypocrite.

How could he lead others to grace while struggling to give it at home?

Naomi noticed the weight he carried.

"You don't have to carry it alone," she told him gently.

"I don't know how to let it go," he admitted. "I keep telling myself I've forgiven him, and then something else happens and the bitterness comes rushing back."

She held his hand. "Forgiveness isn't always a one-time thing. Sometimes, it's daily. Sometimes, it's moment by moment."

Paul began journaling again—something he had stopped when the wounds felt too raw. He wrote prayers, confessions, scriptures, and even unsent letters to Peter.

In one, he wrote:
"I miss you, Peter. Not the version of you who runs and rebels. But the brother who once held my hand crossing the street. I still see him in you. I'm just waiting for you to see him again, too."

Paul knew he couldn't force change. He couldn't drag Peter back to faith or family. But he could fight for his own heart not to grow cold.
He continued praying.
Continued leading.
Continued believing—even if that belief now came with bruises.
Because forgiveness isn't a feeling. It's a decision.
And Paul chose—again and again—to make it.

Grace's Unwavering Faith Despite Her Grief

Grief had become part of Grace's daily rhythm—not just the grief of loss, but the ache of absence, the quiet mourning of a son still living yet so far gone. Every room in the house carried memories of Peter—his laughter, his tantrums, his prayers—and now, each of those memories echoed with the question, "Where did we lose him?"

But even in her sorrow, Grace's faith stood firm. She wasn't in denial. She knew the reality. Peter was lost—in spirit, in direction, in every visible way. But what she also knew, and refused to let go of, was the invisible: God's promise. His mercy. His power to restore.

Grace clung to the scriptures like breath.

"And thy children shall be taught of the Lord; and great shall be the peace of thy children." (Isaiah 54:13)

She wrote that verse on a sticky note and placed it on the mirror in Peter's room.

"For I will pour water upon him that is thirsty, and floods upon the dry ground: I will pour my spirit upon thy seed, and my blessing upon thine offspring." (Isaiah 44:3)

That one stayed in her journal, worn with tears.

Daily, she lit a candle on the dining table, representing her ongoing hope that Peter would return. Not just to their home, but to his purpose. His identity. His God.

There were nights she lay awake, praying in the Spirit when words failed her. There were mornings she knelt by Peter's bed, whispering his name, calling him back in faith.
Samuel often watched her, both in awe and heartbreak.
"How do you keep going?" he asked one day.
Grace smiled gently, eyes moist. "Because I've seen what God can do with ashes. And I won't stop trusting Him with ours."

Church members admired her strength, but they didn't see the private tears. The whispered declarations over Peter's laundry. The late-night worship songs sung softly through trembling lips.
Even Paul, with all his strength, found strength in her.
"You've taught me how to believe when everything says otherwise," he told her.

She squeezed his hand. "That's what faith is, son. Holding the line when it feels like heaven is silent."
Grace refused to mourn like one without hope. Her love for Peter didn't waiver with his choices. Her

faith didn't falter because of the delay. She knew the God who rescued prodigals. She had read the stories. She had lived through storms. And now, she waited—anchored, not in what she saw, but in Who she trusted.

Her grief was real.

But so was her God.

And that made all the difference.

Coming Soon – Volume Two: The Crossroads of Manhood

The choices they made as boys have led them to the edge of something far more dangerous—adulthood. Peter has vanished into the shadows of rebellion, carrying secrets even darker than his silence. Paul is rising in purpose, yet carrying a quiet weight no one fully sees. And while one son builds, the other breaks—and the distance between them grows.

But every path leads somewhere. Every broken heart reaches a threshold. And every prayer whispered in the dark waits for its moment to be answered.

In **Volume Two**, the twins face the defining moments of manhood—love, loyalty, betrayal, ambition, and the pull of destiny. Choices will cost more. Mistakes will cut deeper. And the consequences will echo beyond them.

Will one rise while the other falls? Or is redemption still possible for them both?
The story continues… and the next chapter may change everything.

About the Author

Osoria Asibor is a dynamic storyteller, Christian author, and life coach who writes with a passion for truth, transformation, and timeless values. Born in Nigeria and now based in Canada, he brings a rich cross-cultural perspective to his work—one shaped by faith, family, and the realities of immigrant life.

With a deep understanding of human struggles and the quiet power of choice, Osoria crafts stories that mirror everyday life while inspiring readers to reflect, grow, and draw closer to purpose. His novels are not just entertainment—they are life lessons wrapped in narrative, infused with spiritual depth and practical insight.

A seasoned Bible teacher and mentor, Osoria has dedicated his life to empowering both youth and adults through the written word, public speaking, and ministry. His ability to translate spiritual truths into relatable, emotional experiences has earned him a growing audience of readers who long for fiction that feeds both the mind and the soul.

The Choices We Make is one of many projects in a growing body of work designed to challenge assumptions, stir conviction, and point readers to the One who gives meaning to every path we choose.

He currently lives in Winnipeg, Manitoba, with his beloved wife and children.

Connect with Osoria Asibor:
X: @osoriaasibor
Instagram: @osoriaasibor

www.ingramcontent.com/pod-product-compliance
Lightning Source LLC
Chambersburg PA
CBHW032127160426
43197CB00008B/539